God, Give Me VICTORY over Anger

Thelma Wells

HARVEST HOUSE PUBLISHERS

EUGENE, OREGON

Published in association with D.C. Jacobson & Associates LLC, Lake Oswego, OR 97035, www.dcjacobson.com.

Cover design by Koechel Peterson & Associates, Minneapolis, Minnesota

Cover illustration © 2011 Cartoon Resource

Back cover author photo © Cindi Starr Photography, Colleyville, TX 76034, www.ShootingStarr Photos.com

GOD, GIVE ME VICTORY OVER ANGER
Copyright 2011 by Thelma Wells
Published by Harvest House Publishers
Eugene, Oregon 97402
www.harvesthousepublishers.com

Library of Congress Cataloging-in-Publication Data

Wells, Thelma.
    God, give me victory over anger / Thelma Wells.
        p. cm.
    Includes bibliographical references.
    ISBN 978-0-7369-3919-5 (pbk.)
    ISBN 978-0-7369-4223-2 (eBook)
    1. Anger—Religious aspects—Christianity. I. Title.
BV4627.A5W45 2011
241'.3—dc23

                                                            2011019381

Printed in the United States of America

    11 12 13 14 15 16 17 18 19 20 / BP-NI / 10 9 8 7 6 5 4 3 2 1

This book is dedicated to two men I've been around for years.
They've shown me how to live more Christlike,
managing my anger God's way.

My husband, George Wells, is one of the calmest people I know.
He seldom gets angry and when he does,
he quickly releases it by effectively communicating
with the person or praying about it and letting it go.
(Is he a saint or what?)
He didn't grow up in a hostile family environment.
He had a lot of great role models, worked for himself,
and has the capacity to make lemonade out of lemons.
I thank my husband for teaching me how to stay levelheaded
when things around me turn me upside down.

The other person who has been such a help in writing this book
is my son, George F. Wells. His attention to this project,
which involved supplying great Bible stories
of angry people and his knowledge of anger and
anger-management principles are appreciated.

∞

And "don't sin by letting anger control you."
Don't let the sun go down while you are still angry.

Ephesians 4:26 NLT

Contents

∞

The Saga of the Black-eyed Peas

I was standing at my kitchen counter one day looking at some black-eyed peas that I had put in water to soak overnight. Now, I've been told that you really don't need to soak black-eyed peas overnight before you cook them. But you know, my momma did it, my grandmomma did it, my great-grandmomma did it—so I'm doing it too. I'll always soak them overnight.

Well, these particular peas had soaked for a long time. As I stepped up to my kitchen counter and started looking at them, can you believe it? The Lord started talking to me through the peas! What I saw with these peas is that they had been drowning so long in the water that some of the shells had come off—the skins had peeled. And some of the black-eyed peas were split in half. I noticed too that even though all these black-eyed had similarity in their shapes, some had brown eyes, some had black eyes, some had speckled eyes, some had tiny eyes, and some had big eyes. Soon I noticed there was actually something different about each and every one of them.

Yes, my attention was getting drawn into "the saga of the black-eyed peas." I stood there a long time looking them over. I even held some of them in my hand and let them trickle through my fingers as I examined them. I thought, *You know, this is how people are. We're all human beings, yet each of us is uniquely different from others. We come in different shapes, different colors. We have different thoughts, different attitudes. We're different all over. We even have different DNA. So we're so much alike...yet so different, just like these black-eyed peas.*

Suppose we take and examine each one of us, and put us in hard times that are like drowning waters: the drowning waters of financial troubles, the drowning waters of difficulties in our relationships, the drowning waters of not knowing what we need to know or not having the training we need, the drowning waters of poverty, the drowning waters of sickness and disease. Whatever those drowning waters are for us, through our experience of them, we have opportunities to either change for the better or change for the worse.

And here's what else is true about every one of those situations: We all have an opportunity to get angry about our circumstances or to use those circumstances and change them into something constructive.

Well, let me finish telling you about the black-eyed peas. I kept looking at them as I put them in the water to cook. I added in all the seasonings—salt and pepper and such, and, yes, even chicken broth. And then, when those black-eyed peas cooked, I couldn't tell one black-eyed pea from the other! Now that they were done, they all had a similar consistency. They shared the same color, and they all came out succulent to the tongue.

Isn't that the way it is with life? We drown in situations (or we think we're drowning). But when we're put where we can have some spice and some seasoning and some good stuff...and maybe even a little sugar added in, we can come out with succulent flavor.

We'll be talking in this book about anger. Anger takes different turns, and different phases, and different ways for different reasons. For some of us, the skin comes off our backs and we rage and are upset and go into turmoil, doing things that cause us to be ashamed later and to feel guilty about our response. Some of us just kind of sulk in the water and let apathy capture us. Others of us do what should be done. That is, we keep finding reasons for joy and openly and fully receive all the goodness that comes our way. We allow the circumstances to change our lives for the better.

Oh, I'm aware of many people who are like those black-eyed peas.

They drown in the troubles and the questions and sometimes soak in a skewed view of what reality is. And in those things that are happening in their lives, those things that seem to be so difficult to overcome, they get angry at the drop of a hat. They get upset over things they cannot control. They get resentful about it, and even evil, if you will. They're so bothered by the things they imagine other people are doing to them, when in reality, perhaps those things are really what they're doing to themselves.

All of us have something to be mad about. Everybody I know, everyone I speak to, and everybody who's reading this book—we all have things we can be angry about. Yes we do. But we also have a choice in how we respond.

Anger Postures

Some people are tormented by the emotion of anger for decades. Anger has destroyed relationships, caused lost jobs, ignited violence, ruined health, unraveled marriages, split churches, and so much more. Everybody has experienced it.

Babies cry when they sense it in those around them. Leaders steam and hiss when they experience it. Women talk in their heads when mulling it over. Men get very competitive when they try to deal with it. Parents battle it when dealing with their children. Teenagers rebel in it. And some people even hold on to it like best friends.

Anger is a universal emotion felt by everybody at one time or another. Some people get angry quickly, and then they're over it in a flash. Other people delay their anger until finally they've "had enough," and then they overreact. Still others live in a state of simmering anger for years, sometimes even dying in a state of anger directed against something or someone.

Whatever your stage of anger or the frequency of your anger, this book is devoted to helping you take a look at your "anger posture," to scrutinize your emotional ups and downs. I want to help you see with greater clarity how you react when you're angry. We'll also take a look at how the people around you act when they become angry. We'll explore the possible results of anger and determine if it's worth it to continue in a state of anger for any length of time. Then we'll learn to creatively and constructively deal with anger so it becomes a positive force.

Is Anger a Choice?

As we think about anger, we often have lots of questions. Is anger a choice? Is it something we can't avoid? Is anger ever a good thing? How do our attitudes and methods for dealing with anger help or hurt our relationships? In what ways does anger jade our children and teens? Blemish our work environments? Dismantle our associations and affiliations? Lead us to the point of no going back in disagreements?

In this book I want to help you discover answers to these questions, as well as explore these topics...

- What is anger?

- What are the warning signs of anger?

- What conditions bring on anger?

- Why do we get angry?

- How can we detect anger in our children?

- How can we manage anger in relationships?

- How do we control anger?

- What are the benefits of controlled anger?

- What does God's Word say about anger and sin?

- Does God get angry?

- How can we have victory over anger?

- What are the promises of peace in victory over anger?

What's more, we'll see that even though anger seems to have so many drawbacks, there is an anger that is wrapped in righteousness and victorious results. Perhaps it's a learned behavior taught from the pages of the Holy Bible and practiced by the mighty God of the universe to show us how to live sinless lives when it comes to this powerful emotion.

If you've bottled up anger in your being, it's time to pop the cork. To let the anger spill out into the river of forgiveness. To embrace the cleansing flow. I strongly recommend getting a notebook or journal so you can answer the self-evaluation questions as you go along. This will help you get a lot more out of this book.

So take a deep breath, swallow fresh air, rub away the blurring residue that's in your eyes, and clean out the voice-muffling wax from your ears. Pay attention even though you may have been resisting delving into this often scary area. Get ready to discover how you can push yourself out of the valley of vindictiveness and into the virtue of victory. Remember that everybody becomes angry at one time or the other. It's time to move ahead so you can experience anger and not sin or let it control you. It's time to look at anger with the healthy perspective God intended and respond in ways that honor Him.

Thelma "Mama T" Wells

Part 1

Analyzing Our Anger

1

This Thing Called Anger

I've never considered myself an angry person. But writing this book has caused me to examine myself to see if I'm harboring any anger from past experiences or supressing any in the present. It also prompted me to look at people around me and analyze their anger temperatures. Everywhere I go, whether speaking or hanging out, so many people seem to be angry. It doesn't matter if I'm in the grocery store, mall, post office, airport, church, restaurant, a park—or even just driving down the street—I encounter folks who act like they are angry.

I listen to them talk, and they're angry at the government or the president, their preacher or teacher, their doctor or lawyer, their neighbor or parking attendant, a bus driver or carhop, or at a customer service person or somebody passing by. Have you noticed this too? If you watch people waiting at traffic lights, passing by in their cars, waiting in line for something, or ordering takeout, you can often see angry expressions and actions. In a food establishment, you sit close enough to eavesdrop on conversations and get an earful. I've heard some talk that could have easily earned a page or two in a tabloid magazine. Some people are angry enough to hurt somebody—and you even learn all about how they'd like to do it.

I'm not making a judgment on whether their anger is justified. The fact is, people are mad. Yes, MAD! I wonder if they're mad at themselves and taking it out on the world around them. I wonder if their anger is based on general experience or the harmful commentary we're bombarded with via media (talk radio, television, music, movies, books, and so on). Is their anger fanned into flames simply from talking with other people? Or do they live in a state of anger because of what they've experienced in their lives?

Regardless of ethnicity, age, gender, status, culture, financial state, or educational background, many of the people I come into contact with are downright angry. As I've thought about this epidemic of anger, I had to analyze myself in the process. What angers *me*? What am I mad about and why? When did I become mad about it? Who am I mad at? How can I get over it? When do I plan to release it? And the big question: Am I *sinning* in this anger of mine?

The Scripture says, "'Don't *sin* by letting anger control you.' Don't let the sun go down while you are still angry" (Ephesians 4:26 NLT). *Lord, have mercy! Is this what I'm doing?* And, friend, is this what you are doing?

Justified Anger?

Actually, I don't consider myself a sinner when I'm angry. I often think I *should* be angry for some of the experiences I'm having or have had. There are people I'm *supposed* to be mad at. People who have deceived me, said false things about me, abused me, abandoned me, belittled me, failed me, ganged up on me, hated me, ignored me, joked about me, lied to me, and mismanaged things I've entrusted to them. People have been nasty to me, presented themselves to me falsely, quit on me, railed at me, and acted irate toward me. They stalked me, tattled on me, used me, attacked me, walked away from me, excommunicated me, yelled at me, zeroed out on me.

What have people done to you? Your list may include abuse, accusation, cruelty, destructiveness, enmity, feuding, frustration, hatefulness, spite, contempt, inhospitableness, rudeness, malice, rage, railing, retaliation, lack of cooperation, refusal to admit wrong…and other injurious behaviors.

Wouldn't you think that all these indictments and more are appropriate reasons to be angry? Wouldn't you be justified not only to be angry but to *stay* angry at every one of the people who have hurt you? Wouldn't you think the first part of Ephesians 4:26 is all you need to justify being mad? That it's okay to be angry as long as you don't sin? Do you think you have a *right* to become angry if you want to? Surely you have some rights over your conduct and emotions. After all, God made you an emotional person with a body, soul, and spirit that you can govern. Don't you think so?

Keep reading!

Anger Is...

Do we really know what anger is? Let's take a look at some of the facts to decide if we're angry or not. Let's get a bit academic on the subject.

So what is anger, anyway? We all assume we know what anger is, don't we? In fact, I suspect you've never looked up the word *anger* in a dictionary. And right now you may be thinking, *Why should I look it up in a book? I see it often enough all around me...and even inside me.* But maybe it will be helpful to put the meaning of anger into some objective context. Here's a typical dictionary definition of anger: "a strong emotion; a feeling that is oriented toward some real or supposed grievance."[1] Now isn't it interesting how they put that word *supposed* in there? Could it be that a significant amount of our anger is about "supposed" grievances rather than "real" grievances?

Here's another definition: "Anger is an emotion related to one's psychological interpretation of having been offended, wronged, or denied, and a tendency to undo that by retaliation."[2] This one brings in the very real danger of anger. We don't always just sit and let it stew in our minds and hearts. We go for *retaliation*. We *want* to do some damage; we *want* somebody to suffer. It's so easy to want to lash out at someone for the anger we feel. It happens all the time, doesn't it?

Back in the early Middle Ages, the great scholar Thomas Aquinas wrote much about anger. At one point he simply defined *anger* as "a desire for vengeance." He went on to say that "hatred is far worse and graver than anger."[3]

Losing Control

A long time ago, in the early years of my marriage, I stewed in a pot of anger toward my husband. You see, I entered marriage with expectations that I soon discovered were unreasonable and wouldn't be met. My fairy-tale fantasy of our never disagreeing with each other and the two of us meeting all of each other's needs quickly faded into the recesses of my mind and heart. I thought I'd been fooled and betrayed. The anger I felt toward George was increased because I'd seen women experience similar situations and determined it would never happen to me. So I wanted to retaliate. I wanted to hurt him! I was losing control. I became irrational and irritable. I did and said things I later regretted.

Yes, people often undergo changes in their personality when they get angry. They often let themselves lose control. Like me, they let their actions and words become irrational and later will want to go back to undo and unsay. When we get angry, we can experience annoyance, frustration, desire for violence, and irritation.

Are you getting enough of this picture to understand what we're tackling when talking about anger? Just thinking about it heightens my blood pressure! Does this discussion take you back to some incidents in your past that you would rather forget about?

Isn't it powerful that we can stop right this minute and pray to God to remove the stain and sting of past negative incidences that haunt us from time to time? That we can give them to the Lord and leave them with Him right now?

> *Father in heaven, past incidences of my expressed and unexpressed anger creep up on me sometimes, and I remember how I reacted to what I decided to get angry about. Some people were damaged—and I was damaged too.*
>
> *Here I am. Please forgive me. Wash me of my sinful responses to anger and the guilt that has lingered.*
>
> *I need You, Jesus, to cover me with Your forgiving blood and take away the sting of my transgressions.*
>
> *Thanks for hearing and answering this prayer. In Your name I pray. Amen.*

A Strategy That Works

As Christians, we're going to deal with minor irritations, frustrations, and annoyances as long as we're in our physical bodies. But our feelings can be contained and controlled by the grace of God so they don't advance into the realm of becoming cross, upset, or rageful.

Now, I'm a Christian, but I remember years ago when I was not as anointed as I am today. Let's go again to my early marriage days. One day as my husband was talking on the telephone, I thought I overheard a woman's voice responding. It could have been a relative or a family friend—all I heard was a woman's voice. And George seemed to be talking to her with affection even though I was in the room!

When George hung up, I asked him who he was talking to. He told me. However, my imagination had already run wild, and I didn't believe him. I started fussing and accusing him of talking to someone he didn't want me to know about. The harder he tried to explain, the madder I got. I walked out of the room, slammed the door, and started to think about what I could do to hurt him back.

He was crushed by my suspicion and response. Later that day the lady called back. (As you probably guessed, by then I was monitoring all incoming phone calls.) When I answered the phone, this woman— George's cousin—said, "Hey, girl, I was in a hurry and didn't speak to you when I called earlier, but I need to talk to George again." She mentioned what they had been discussing and asked, "Is he still there?"

Egg was on my face and shame was in my mind. My husband had told me the truth, but my insecurity overshadowed the place of reason. I had to go to George, eat my words, apologize, and bandage both our wounds.

Do you think I was sinning when I behaved like that? I do. I was operating on assumptions, thinking evil, and falsely accusing my husband. I was irate and willing to hold a grudge. I was even scheming about how to get revenge. I was up in the air about something that was baseless and grossly unfair. Do I feel bad about that? You bet I do. Even now, more than three decades later, the memory of how I mistrusted and embarrassed my husband (let alone myself) still stings in the inner parts of my being.

Yes, there were a number of times that George had issues that caused agitation and frustration in both of us. You see, it takes two to argue. One day my husband and I were discussing life and its dimensions, and George proposed a strategy for handling our conflicts that sounded reasonable, though I wondered if it would work. He suggested this: "Let's promise each other that we will never again go to sleep angry at each other."

That sounded appropriate...even though I was skeptical about whether it would work. But I was willing to try. That idea was posed in 1974, and I must say that from that time until now, we have not gone to sleep angry with each other. We have had some sleepless nights. The good thing about this is that one of us will humble ourselves and begin the conversation to resolve our differences. Praise God for healthy communication!

I believe that irritation, frustration, annoyance, and being cross are not sins. But the line is crossed when we get mad and go into a rage. Not being willing to listen to reason, getting indignant, pointing fingers, and being uncontrollably irate is never a good witness for a Christian to exhibit to a world filled with chaos and questions, a world looking for hope and solace. Rage is not a Christlike characteristic.

There are people by nature who are meek and mild. They aren't given to outward rage. However, they often fume and boil inside until their pot boils over. Then, even though they're Christians, when they've had enough, *they've had enough* and blow sky high.

What do the Scriptures offer us about this aspect of our conduct? Listen to these words from the apostle Paul:

> So I say, walk by the Spirit, and you will not gratify the desires of the flesh. For the flesh desires what is contrary to the Spirit, and the Spirit what is contrary to the flesh. They are in conflict with each other, so that you are not to do whatever you want. But if you are led by the Spirit, you are not under the law.
>
> The acts of the flesh are obvious: sexual immorality, impurity and debauchery; idolatry and witchcraft; hatred, discord, jealousy, fits of rage, selfish ambition, dissensions,

factions and envy; drunkenness, orgies, and the like. I warn you, as I did before, that those who live like this will not inherit the kingdom of God.

But the fruit of the Spirit is love, joy, peace, forbearance, kindness, goodness, faithfulness, gentleness and self-control. Against such things there is no law (Galatians 5:16-23 NIV).

Did you get it? We Christians have a code of conduct that delineates our sinful state from our Christlike state. Recognizing this difference and comprehending it is really not hard to do—just check the Book, God's Word!

Different Responses

No two people are alike. Even our children aren't alike. And this extends to our emotional responses. We all respond differently in our anger.

I know someone very close to me who is a mild-mannered sweetheart. She seldom raises her voice, even when she's not being treated appropriately. She just takes it and takes it even though she realizes that things are not right. She chooses to let people go on doing what they're doing until finally it begins to nag on her. If it continues, she begins to stew with anger, playing the irritation over and over in her head. The strain multiplies as she rehearses the offenses. She becomes more and more angry.

This person runs a successful business, and too many people have taken advantage of her kindness. When her pot boils over, I've seen her set people's belongings on the front porch of her establishment, and then she calls them to come and get their stuff. She releases them from any obligation to her in the future. This happens after she has talked to them about the problem, warned them, given them chances to get things right, and shown them what they need to do to correct things. One time when she worked in another establishment with a partner, she was again being used over and over. She became so angry that she took everything out of the physical location, including the lightbulbs!

Is that sinning? Perhaps. However, I don't think her anger is the sin. Reprimands or resolutions aren't sins either because there are consequences to our actions. However, I'm sure that one action would be sin—not forgiving the people who didn't do right. The sin would be holding a grudge and mulling over or nursing the anger for days, weeks, months, years, and even decades.

When you feel harmed, don't go to the person arrogantly, spewing with poison like a snake. Instead, be prayerful and humble in your approach. Jesus said,

> If your brother or sister sins, go and point out their fault, just between the two of you. If they listen to you, you have won them over. But if they will not listen, take one or two others along, so that "every matter may be established by the testimony of two or three witnesses." If they still refuse to listen, tell it to the church; and if they refuse to listen even to the church, treat them as you would a pagan or a tax collector (Matthew 18:15-17 NIV).

So the first step is to pray and get God's okay for what you want to do. Then you can approach the offender.

In Your Own Words

Think more about your own definition of anger. How does anger affect you physically, emotionally, and spiritually? Write down your answers to the following questions. Then mark whether your response is a reaction or an action.

- What different stages do you recognize in your own experiences of anger?

- At what point does it seem that your reactions might become sinful?

- Is there anything that qualifies as positive anger, good anger, or healthy anger? If yes, how would you define or describe this good anger? (For example, some people who become angry start projects or movements, such as MADD—Mothers Against Drunk Drivers—to help change situations.)

❊ Is this a new way of thinking about anger for you? If yes, in what way?

∞

Would you like to pray for a deeper understanding of your anger right now?

> *Lord, I want to know myself better and to understand who I am when I'm angry. Do I follow the principles taught in Your Word, the Bible? Or do I act like a stranger to the Word of God and You? Teach me Your ways so I can represent You in all I feel, think, and do. Thanks. Amen.*

The World's First Anger

Right now I'm sitting here wondering, *What is the first incident of anger mentioned in the Bible?* Duh! It's in the story of Adam and Eve.

We don't have a clue to how long this first couple had been living and loving in the most beautiful, peaceful, *awesome* place in the universe before Eve succumbed to the deception of the adversary. But can't you imagine how God felt when Eve and Adam ate the forbidden fruit of the "tree of the knowledge of good and evil?"

God gave these two human beings authority over everything in the garden. Adam named every animal. They had gourmet meals every day and didn't have to cook them. They had crystal-clear, unfiltered, delicious water to drink and 100 percent real fruit juice to drink. The fish weren't contaminated, and the bread was baked fresh daily and naturally. The beams from the sun provided the perfect temperature moment by moment, and the stars and moon gazed upon Adam and Eve in the perfectly pleasant twilight each evening. Birds sang like symphonies in the trees, and the turtledoves showed them how to romance. Never had it rained—just a cooling mist that sprang up through the lush grass and flourished as needed to keep the plants colorful and fruitful. Oh my, it was heaven on earth! Adam and Eve were permitted to eat, drink, and be merry, enjoying the lavish abundance of everything in this utopia. The only thing to avoid was one specific tree.

I surmise Adam and Eve may have lived in Eden for thousands of years before ego got the best of them. And then Eve opened up to the sinister voice of the greatest liar of all times—Satan. He persuaded her to taste the fruit from the forbidden tree in the center of the garden. Adam quickly followed Eve's example.

Afterward, when it was accountability time before their Creator, they each accused somebody else of making them disobey. Don't you think God was very disappointed and righteously angry? And He certainly was mad at Satan. God got mad at all three of the guilty ones—Eve, Adam, and Satan.

God punished the serpent by cursing snakes. They would forever crawl on their bellies in the dust and be enemies of mankind.

And God disciplined Adam and Eve, and all their descendants, by making life hard. They would no longer live in a perfect world like they had known in the garden of Eden. Men would have to struggle, work, and sweat for their existence and that of their families. Women would have pain in childbearing and be ruled by their husbands.

Adam and Eve were thrown out of the beautiful garden forever. They lived a new and toilsome existence.

Was God justified in being angry and punishing them for their disobedience? Of course He was! He forgave them, but there are consequences to wrong behavior. He gave them another chance at life by moving them away from the perfect world to a place of pain and difficult situations. And God looked forward and sent Jesus to restore humanity's relationship with Him. What grace and mercy!

In Your Own Words

❉ What lessons on anger do you find in this story?

❉ What lessons on sinning or not sinning do you find in this story for your life?

❋ How would you have handled this case of gross disobedience?

Anger in the Scriptures

Bible scholars point out that there are a number of Hebrew words used in the Old Testament to convey the idea of anger—human anger and God's anger. These words are quite interesting in their derivation and connotations.

The noun *'ap* (occurring 210 times or so in the Old Testament) "portrays flaring nostrils and emphasizes the emotional impact of anger."[4] Do your nostrils flare when you get angry? If you're not sure, look in a mirror the next time you're really mad about something. In Hebrew this word comes from a root word that originally meant "nose," which over time evolved into a word for "trembling" and "snorting," and later came to mean "anger."

Then there's *hemah* (used about 115 times in the Old Testament). It implies "heat, poison, venom, rage." A related word, *haron* (used 33 times), carries the similar meaning of "burning." We all know how anger heats us up and how somebody needs to "cool off" when anger is in control.

Ebrah (used 24 times) implies "an overflow" or "excess," as in blowing your top.

The Hebrew noun *qesep* (used 28 times) and related words are said to be "perhaps the strongest terms" for anger in the Old Testament, usually translated in English as "wrath." I find it particularly significant that this term "focuses attention on the relational damage done when one party has said or done something that causes hot anger or deep displeasure."[5] Relational damage is such a tragic outcome of so much of our anger.

These are just some of the many Hebrew words for anger in the Old Testament. The words themselves don't tell us if anger is either right or wrong, and they don't explain God's anger. All we know is that there is anger in this world. Anger is *real*. And you don't have to take my word for it. Look at your children and relatives. Turn on the television, read the tabloids, talk to your neighbors, attend church, be affiliated with a group of any kind. Drive down the street and observe traffic. Linger in hospitals and rehabilitation centers. Listen to those who have been laid off their jobs. Watch for friction on playgrounds. Observe the staff as well as customers in business establishments. Anger is all around you. Don't be shocked when you start noticing how much there is! Anger *exists*—in ourselves and around us. We live with anger.

In contrast to the wide variety of Hebrew words for anger found in the Old Testament, when we come to the Greek language of the New Testament, we find two basic terms used to signify anger. Apparently they both mean pretty much the same thing. That's why when the Old Testament, written in Hebrew, was translated into Greek to make the Scripture version "Septuagint," which was widely used in the days of Jesus and the early church, the two Greek terms were used fairly interchangeably to translate all the Hebrew terms for anger. I suppose this goes to show that when it comes to anger, everybody seems to recognize exactly what it is even when it's called by various names. (This is just like we do in English, with *anger, rage, fury, wrath, temper, ire, vehemence,* and so forth.) There's something about anger that's universally recognized. We all get the picture.

Or do we really?

In the pages to come, we'll continue to study anger more closely in the Scriptures to make sure we know exactly what we're talking about and what we're dealing with.

In Your Own Words

❧ After going through this chapter, how would you define *anger*?

Anger Is About Control

In the words of one of my closest and most special friends, "Anger is a power struggle for control and power over the other person(s). It's actually ignorance and a lack of understanding of what's going on around the person who is angry. It's control versus power. The angry person is confused. His or her aim is to destroy something, to show someone that 'I'm in control of my situation.'"

People stay angry because they don't understand what's going on around them, and that's confusing and frustrating. I believe that arrogance, false pride, haughtiness, and self-centeredness have these people standing guard and putting on a show of false power to cover their foggy understanding. Can you relate?

In Your Own Words

❀ Do you agree or disagree with my friend's "control versus power" explanation of anger? Why or why not?

❀ Who in the Bible reminds you of this kind of power struggle? Name them and summarize their stories.

∽

Let's ask God to help us open our hearts and eyes to His truths about our anger.

> *Lord, help me take a good look at myself as I open my eyes to Your truths. Please open my ears to hear Your Word speak to me clearly as I deal with my anger and hang-ups. In Jesus' name. Amen.*

Jonah's Power Struggle

This concept of a power and control struggle reminds me of the prophet Jonah. See if you agree. Here are the details straight from his book in the Bible:

> Now the word of the LORD came to Jonah the son of Amittai, saying, "Arise, go to Nineveh, that great city, and cry out against it; for their wickedness has come up before Me."
> But Jonah arose to flee to Tarshish from the presence of the LORD. He went down to Joppa, and found a ship going to Tarshish; so he paid the fare, and went down into

it, to go with them to Tarshish from the presence of the LORD.

But the LORD sent out a great wind on the sea, and there was a mighty tempest on the sea, so that the ship was about to be broken up. Then the mariners were afraid; and every man cried out to his god, and threw the cargo that was in the ship into the sea, to lighten the load. But Jonah had gone down into the lowest parts of the ship, had lain down, and was fast asleep.

So the captain came to him, and said to him, "What do you mean, sleeper? Arise, call on your God; perhaps your God will consider us, so that we may not perish."

And they said to one another, "Come, let us cast lots, that we may know for whose cause this trouble has come upon us." So they cast lots, and the lot fell on Jonah. Then they said to him, "Please tell us! For whose cause is this trouble upon us? What is your occupation? And where do you come from? What is your country? And of what people are you?"

So he said to them, "I am a Hebrew; and I fear the LORD, the God of heaven, who made the sea and the dry land."

Then the men were exceedingly afraid, and said to him, "Why have you done this?" For the men knew that he fled from the presence of the LORD, because he had told them. Then they said to him, "What shall we do to you that the sea may be calm for us?"—for the sea was growing more tempestuous.

And he said to them, "Pick me up and throw me into the sea; then the sea will become calm for you. For I know that this great tempest is because of me."

Nevertheless the men rowed hard to return to land, but they could not, for the sea continued to grow more tempestuous against them. Therefore they cried out to the LORD and said, "We pray, O LORD, please do not let us perish for this man's life, and do not charge us with innocent blood; for You, O LORD, have done as it pleased You."

So they picked up Jonah and threw him into the sea, and the sea ceased from its raging. Then the men feared the LORD exceedingly, and offered a sacrifice to the LORD and took vows (Jonah 1:1-16 NKJV).

There are a lot of angry people in this story! God sent Jonah on a mission trip to evangelize some people who desperately needed saving, but Jonah hated the people there and chose to go in a different direction. That was a dumb mistake! God was frustrated with His prophet—and I don't blame Him. Jonah was being disrespectful of the instructions from almighty God. Didn't he know that God knew what he was up to?

God sent a hurricane, and the men on that ship got scared and angry. They knew things were calm before Jonah came aboard, so they interrogated the man and found out he was a prophet. At Jonah's request, they threw him overboard.

Meanwhile, Jonah was mad at himself for causing this havoc. But the story doesn't end there!

Now the LORD had prepared a great fish to swallow Jonah. And Jonah was in the belly of the fish three days and three nights. Then Jonah prayed to the LORD his God from the fish's belly. And he said:

"I cried out to the LORD because of my affliction, and He answered me. Out of the belly of Sheol I cried, and You heard my voice. For You cast me into the deep, into the heart of the seas, and the floods surrounded me; all Your billows and Your waves passed over me.

"Then I said, 'I have been cast out of Your sight; yet I will look again toward Your holy temple.' The waters surrounded me, even to my soul; the deep closed around me; weeds were wrapped around my head. I went down to the moorings of the mountains; the earth with its bars closed behind me forever; yet You have brought up my life from the pit, O LORD, my God.

"When my soul fainted within me, I remembered the LORD; and my prayer went up to You, into Your holy temple. Those who regard worthless idols forsake their own Mercy. But I will sacrifice to You with the voice of thanksgiving; I will pay what I have vowed. Salvation is of the LORD."

So the LORD spoke to the fish, and it vomited Jonah onto dry land (1:17–2:10).

Jonah knew God had a perfect right to be angry with him. But still Jonah prayed for mercy and got it. Jonah was given a second chance, a fresh start on dry ground.

Now the word of the LORD came to Jonah the second time, saying, "Arise, go to Nineveh, that great city, and preach to it the message that I tell you."

So Jonah arose and went to Nineveh, according to the word of the LORD. Now Nineveh was an exceedingly great city, a three-day journey in extent. And Jonah began to enter the city on the first day's walk. Then he cried out and said, "Yet forty days, and Nineveh shall be overthrown!"

So the people of Nineveh believed God, proclaimed a fast, and put on sackcloth, from the greatest to the least of them. Then word came to the king of Nineveh; and he arose from his throne and laid aside his robe, covered himself with sackcloth and sat in ashes. And he caused it to be proclaimed and published throughout Nineveh by the decree of the king and his nobles, saying,

"Let neither man nor beast, herd nor flock, taste anything; do not let them eat, or drink water. But let man and beast be covered with sackcloth, and cry mightily to God; yes, let every one turn from his evil way and from the violence that is in his hands. Who can tell if God will turn and relent, and turn away from *His fierce anger*, so that we may not perish?" (Jonah 3:1-9).

The people understood that God was intensely angry with them, and they had sense enough to respond in the right way. God saw their works, that they turned from their evil way, and He relented from the disaster He'd said He would bring upon them. He did not do it (Jonah 3:10).

More mercy from God! And yet look at this:

> But it displeased Jonah exceedingly, and *he became angry.* So he prayed to the LORD, and said, "Ah, LORD, was not this what I said when I was still in my country? Therefore I fled previously to Tarshish; for I know that You are a gracious and merciful God, slow to anger and abundant in lovingkindness, One who relents from doing harm. Therefore now, O LORD, please take my life from me, for it is better for me to die than to live!"
>
> Then the LORD said, "Is it right for you to be angry?"
>
> So Jonah went out of the city and sat on the east side of the city. There he made himself a shelter and sat under it in the shade, till he might see what would become of the city. And the LORD God prepared a plant and made it come up over Jonah, that it might be shade for his head to deliver him from his misery. So Jonah was very grateful for the plant.
>
> But as morning dawned the next day God prepared a worm, and it so damaged the plant that it withered. And it happened, when the sun arose, that God prepared a vehement east wind; and the sun beat on Jonah's head, so that he grew faint. Then he wished death for himself, and said, "It is better for me to die than to live."
>
> Then God said to Jonah, "*Is it right for you to be angry* about the plant?"
>
> And he said, "It is right for me to be angry, even to death!"
>
> But the LORD said, "You have had pity on the plant for which you have not labored, nor made it grow, which came up in a night and perished in a night. And should I not pity Nineveh, that great city, in which are more than

one hundred and twenty thousand persons who cannot discern between their right hand and their left—and much livestock?" (Jonah 4:1-11 NKJV).

Let's cut to the chase. Jonah was disobedient, prejudiced, arrogant, judgmental, frustrated, headstrong, ignorant, vengeful, and (have I stated this before?) stupid. The men on the ship were angry with him, the whale that swallowed him couldn't stomach him, God couldn't trust him, and the people to whom he was sent didn't like him. This saga is filled with complications. In fact, it reminds me of those black-eyed peas that soaked overnight and lost their shells—fragmented and split.

But the story ends with God winning because His will had already won the victory. How did He win? God has the last word! If we believe wholeheartedly in Him and His supremacy in our situation, we would not be so easily angered at anything. Jonah finally had to humble himself to the will of God. I'm convinced that one way to have victory over anger is to obey God and do His will. That cuts out a lot of frustration. Let's pray!

> Lord, I get so tired of being frustrated and upset over things I don't want to do and things I have no control over. Please help me do Your will. Release me from my selfish bondage of wanting to do things my way. Thanks for helping me, Lord. Amen.

2

Causes, Trigger Points, and Warning Signs

I've been thinking about anger and me. I wonder why I get so upset with people I really, really love. What are the main triggers? What sets my anger ablaze?

Afraid of the Unknown

I think one of the main triggers is something I understand better now because I can look back on the times I was worried about the possibility of losing my husband. When George became extremely ill, I didn't realize how sick he really was so I didn't comprehend what the consequences might be. And because I wasn't sure of what was going on with him and didn't understand why he was reacting the way he was, I felt overwhelming fear. I didn't know how to deal with that either. I got very irritable. I would suddenly become very angry, even at the things he would say that were totally innocent or nonconfrontive.

Now, with hindsight, I know I wasn't really angry at him. No, I was *afraid* because I didn't know what was going to happen. And my irritability rose because I thought, *Lord, what am I going to do? Am I going to have to take care of him the rest of his life? What is going to happen to me and our family? And what about my career?*

As I think about that, I can easily imagine that when you and I find ourselves getting agitated, one of the reasons could be simply that we don't know the future. God knows our emotions (and thank Him for giving us emotions!). And I am so grateful that He had an answer to my frightened irritability during George's illness.

That day when worry reared its ugly head, I went to an elegant luncheon given to honor one of my "daughters in the ministry" who has her own outreach for Christ. She had lost her husband to cancer a few years prior and in her acceptance speech she revealed her heart. She said that in her lonely, saddened state God led her to a scripture. First Kings 17:17-24 tells about the starvation of a widow and her son, and how she reluctantly followed the prophet Elijah's instructions and discovered God would provide enough meal and oil when she used the small amount of leftovers in her possession for His purposes. Dr. Sheila Bailey, of Sheila B's Ministries in Dallas, Texas, gave me the secret of recovering from anger and doubt in times of loss: "Live out of the leftovers that God has provided you!"

Let me teach a minute so you'll get what I'm talking about.

You may have grief and anger over loss (it doesn't matter what kind). Today is your day to discover the leftovers in your life and begin to recover your heart and mind by appreciating what you have. What's left in your life when loss or tragedy or bankruptcy is eminent and you can't see what's ahead of you? That's what I started evaluating. If I were to lose my best friend, lover, supporter, confidant, caregiver, father of my children, champion of my family, what would be my leftovers?

My life, health, strength, memories, other family members, friends, community, church, activities, travel opportunities, dreams, photos and videos of great times together, laughter, old jokes, favorite pieces of furniture, past conversations, favorite foods and eating places, hopes, peace and contentment, his legacy continued through his children and grandchildren, and the list goes on.

When I look at George now and the toll the aging process is taking, instead of being angry or hurt because of it, I find myself praising God for this life we've shared of more than 50 years (half a century!). I know when this life on earth ends, George's life will continue with Jesus, and one day I'll join both of them and that life will never end. Yes, I know

Jesus said, "At the resurrection people will neither marry nor be given in marriage," but we'll still be together! (See Matthew 22:30 NIV.) Of course, George may outlive me…and then the roles will be reversed!

Oh! I want to shout now. "Hallelujah! Thank You, Jesus!" Life is a vapor moving through an open gate—and that gate will never grow old and never end. I can no longer be angry at life and the decay it brings when my citizenship is not on earth and neither is my husband's. We are passing through to the New Jerusalem, where there will never be a thought of loss or aging, hurting or suffering, and the meal in the barrel will never give out. "Hallelujah one more time!"

Let me just stop right here and pray for you if you're grieving and angry over a loss.

> *Heavenly Father, I come to You on behalf of this reader who is grieving over a loss and struggling with anger. I'm so glad You understand her loss and her anger. Thank You for not being mad at her for feeling the way she does.*
>
> *I'm so glad You brought me out of the darkness of my anger and fear and sent me heavenly encouragement through a woman whom I love and respect. You had her open her mouth about her experiences to give me hope and help in a difficult time. Because of that, You enable me to help others. From Your heart through my heart, God, I offer hope and help to this woman who is hurting, grieving, and feeling hopeless. In the name of Jesus, please massage her heart so she can hear and adhere to Your message of solace. Encourage her to "live out of what's left," realizing there is much more left than meets her eyes.*
>
> *Thank You, God, for bringing her out of despair and anger to a brighter life of peace and contentment. Amen.*

Feeling Slighted or Bothered

Another reason I tend to get angry is when I feel someone is belittling me. For example, if I tell somebody something, and she replies, "Well, I don't think that's true. I don't believe you're right about that,"

that irritates me, and the longer I think about what she said, the angrier I become. My inner response? "I'm telling you the truth, and you're questioning my integrity. How dare you!"

I also get angry when I get interrupted a lot while I'm working on a major project. I know life happens. There are always interruptions. They're coming at us all the time. But when I'm really into something, really working hard, and I'm interrupted, it's hard to stay relaxed about it. Is that true for you?

I know the famous words of Eleanor Roosevelt: "No one can make you feel inferior without your consent." She was right about that. It's my choice whether I let the scorn or contempt of others make me feel slighted or insulted. It takes my cooperation. I understand that. I know that anger is a choice. I can decide whether to be angry or not to be angry. But deciding to be angry often seems like such a quick and effortless choice! Life is full of choices, and the choices we make determine the conditions of our heart and the stability of our minds. That's one good reason I wear a bumblebee pin every day. It reminds me that the choices I make will determine how high I fly in life. These are the choices that determine whether I achieve victory. Yes, there have been times when I haven't made wise choices, and those moments caused me grief.

In Your Own Words

❀ Have you made unwise choices that you regret? Explain.

❀ How did you handle the situation?

❀ What were the results?

A Dark Visitation

Let me tell you about a dark encounter I experienced.

I think my biggest pet peeve is when someone is disrespecting me for any reason. Now, I don't get disrespected very often, but over the years one person has put me down more often than I like to remember.

I do recall one occasion that changed my life. On that particular day I was having a telephone conversation with that person. I was trying to be nice, trying to encourage her, trying to help her. She started abusing me by saying rude things and using profanity. She acted really, really crazy—lunatic crazy.

As I said, this wasn't the first time this person had done that with me. There had been instances going back for a long, long time, through different seasons, different times, and for various reasons. But this particular time, I'd had it. You know what I mean. Sometimes we just reach rock bottom in dealing with a situation. And I had reached it with this individual. For months and months and years and years, I had taken her abuse. But now I decided, *This is it. I've had it! She has killed my respect and my love for her. She can just hang it up. I don't want to be bothered with her anymore. I don't want to see her anymore. I don't want to have anything to do with her!*

So I said, "I don't want you to be around me. I don't want you coming to my house. I don't want to see you. I don't want to talk with you. In fact, you can take a long walk off a short pier!"

I really felt that way. I was so injured. My heart was aching and breaking. The audacity of this person whom I had been really good to all this time and who was now being so ugly to me! The very idea that she would respond to me with such verbal abuse made me mad. It was infuriating.

I stayed in that general frame of mind—as mad as a wet hen—for about seven days. And this was years after I'd promised God I would never hate again. Yes, *hate*. That was what I'd felt before...and what I was feeling now. The anger was almost debilitating. (And I laugh when I think about it now because seven is the "number of completion" in the Bible.) Let me tell you what happened on the seventh day. For all that week I had been harboring this anger—thinking about it, feeling detestable about it, and almost hating what this individual had done to me. I almost hated this individual. I even entertained rejoicing at her death. That is *sin!* And I had it bad. (I am not proud of this.)

It was four in the morning, and I was out of town at a conference. I had the most sinister visitation I've ever experienced. I know it was a demon from hell—I know that! Maybe you don't know much about demons or how they operate, but the Bible says they are real. I encourage you to watch out and do right so you can avoid what I experienced, okay? Demons are around. In fact, their reality is called the demonic dimension, and if you study that, you'll see there are even categories of demons—powers, principalities, wickedness in high places, witchcraft. The devil's minions operate in the world even now. The way to avoid an encounter with them is to obey God and plead the blood of Jesus over yourself and those you love.

Well, I don't know where this demon came from that morning. I just know it was a sinister, perverted power that tormented me. And when it came, it was something that had never happened to me before. Never—and I never want it to happen again.

When the demon attacked me through my dreams, I woke up startled, shocked, and afraid. As I was waking up, I didn't even know what kind of stupor I was in, but I knew that a sinister spirit had tried to enter my body. I couldn't even speak the name of Jesus clearly. I said, "Jeeeessssssss...Jeeeeeeessssss...Jessssssssss." After trying to call His name several times, I finally got out "Jeeeesus! Jeeeesus!" And I cried, "God, what is this? Help me!" I began to plead the blood of Jesus because that's what I know to do. Satan cannot stand against the blood of Jesus. Demons flee when the blood of Jesus is talked about and claimed. So I pleaded His blood and the demon left me alone. But I continued to pray. *God, what is this? Help me understand what just happened. This is awful! This is terrible! I feel so bad, so unclean.*

And the Lord spoke to me through my spirit. He said, "How can you stand before people and tell them to forgive those who have hurt them when *you* won't forgive? How many times have I forgiven you? *How dare you not forgive!* If you don't forgive this person, I will snatch your anointing from you!"

Jesus was telling me *to live what I preach*. He prompted me. He told me. He urged me. He said I had to forgive this person I was so angry toward. I didn't have a choice in this matter. If I wanted God to continue teaching me His way and anointing me for His service, I'd better get my heart in tune with His.

Jesus told me to stop harboring the hatred and the hurt—and the self-centeredness too. I guess that's maybe what it really amounted to. He reminded me how He had told me—as He has told all of us through His Word—that I am to forgive over and over and over again. What did He say to Peter when he asked how many times he should forgive? "I do not say to you seven times, but seventy times seven" (Matthew 18:21). What Jesus was saying was that we are to forgive that many times every day if necessary. That's how often we are to forgive whatever another person has done to hurt us. Seventy times seven! Don't count the times someone has hurt you. *Just do what God says to do.* Forgive that person. Over and over again if necessary. That's how we don't sin when we're angry. Be obedient!

Wow, that's hard to live up to, isn't it? And it's even harder when we experience God chastising us about it!

And so, at four-something in the morning, I got up and sent a text message to the person I was angry at. I told her, "I have asked God to help me forgive you." I was committed to forgiving because of the sinister visitation God allowed me to experience, because of God's forgiveness of me, and because He chastised me. And I told that person, "I want you to know that I release you from the situation I believe you caused. It really doesn't matter who caused it. The fact is, my reaction to it was ungodly, and I apologize to you."

I also apologized to God. And I promised God that I would not allow myself to get angry like that again. You see, once the door is open to anger, bitterness, and frustration, it gives Satan an entry to come in and do whatever he wants. When our minds are riddled with a lack of forgiveness, Satan tries to take advantage of our confusion.

Yes, I was on my knees and asking God to forgive me. And when I finished praying, I wrote this person a longer text message. And this time it was not all about what I felt this person had done; rather, it was about the tender, loving mercy of God.

I knew that sometimes this particular person was very angry, very bitter. Because hurting people tend to harm other people, I think that was why I was hurt so badly. I had been hurt many, many times by this person because she is a seriously hurting and hurtful individual. But I could say, with God's grace and mercy, "I forgive you." I felt that for-giveness in my heart, and I meant it in my mind. *I forgive!*

Wow! I got up and put praise music on. I felt the power of God anointing me again because I had been obedient to do what I'd decided I never wanted to do—forgive that person. Remember, I said I never wanted to see her again. But when God washes us clean, when God delivers us, He doesn't do it halfway! *Thank You, Jesus!* He goes all the way, even into the nooks and crannies!

What a powerful, merciful, grace-filled God we serve! And I'm glad I know Him enough to understand when He's chastising me and what He's saying to me. Then I follow through on His plan through His mercy and strength.

I went on to think, *How many times have I hurt God? Yet He doesn't get mad at me and throw me out with the dishwater. He never tells me, "Don't talk to Me anymore." He doesn't say to me, "Get out of My face." He doesn't say, "Get out of My house and don't come around." All He says is one word: "Forgiven."*

Let me teach a little bit here. I've used the word "anointing" a num-ber of times so far. It literally means "to smear or rub with oil, and by implication to consecrate for office or religious service." Because God has called me to write books and speak about Him everywhere I go, He has consecrated my life for religious service in His name. It's such a privilege to serve Him. Do you want to do that too? Let's pray for com-plete forgiveness and anointing.

> *Heavenly Father, I want and need Your anointing in my life because that anointing breaks the yoke of bondage and bur-den. Sometimes I get so caught up in me and how I want to be treated that I become too impressed with me. I lose perspective on who You are. Please forgive me. Help me be slow to anger. Help me act lovingly to all people. Amen.*

Facing Our Fears

It's hard to look at ourselves the way God does. We don't want to know all that He knows about our lives (which is everything. *Yes, everything!*). But let's ask ourselves this question: "Why am I angry?" Honesty is the best policy here. Check your heart more closely than you check your refrigerator when you clean it out. Do you know what I mean? When you clean out your refrigerator, you may find penicillin growing on the sour cream, crust from milk droppings, spoiled milk in the bottle, once-crisp vegetables that have turned to mush, jelly jars that once had sweet stuff in them but now it's a hardened mess, and a lot of garbage that should have been thrown out a long time ago. Now, think about that in relation to your life and your heart.

We've filled our lives with all sorts of garbage. We've created hazardous materials and waste. So shed light on the hidden spots. Dig in and clean out all the disgusting and rotting material. When we approach anger this way, it brings us ever closer to Christ and to a deeper relationship with Him. Dishonesty, however, leads us in exactly the opposite direction.

Let me explain through example. I was having a lot of pain and discomfort in my legs at one time. I used home remedies to get some relief, but nothing was working well. My wonderful friend NiJo recognized the hurting look on my face. After observing me for a while, she sent me to her doctor with a promise that he would be able to figure out what the problem was.

She was right. After a lengthy consultation and thorough physical, he asked me what I was mad about.

I was shocked! *Me? Mad?*

"I'm not mad," I asserted. "What do you mean?"

He then asked what I was disgusted about.

I was taken by surprise. Was I really angry, mad, and disgusted?

He was kind enough to allow me time to think. It didn't take long for me to remember who and what had me tied up in knots. I confessed that I was upset and explained the situation.

The doctor treated me. I don't remember how or when the pain subsided, I just remember that I uncovered the source of my discomfort and experienced relief. Since that day, I question my heart condition when discomfort arises in my body. I've begun to see the places my emotions hide out in and make choices that help heal my soul.

Anger Has Patterns

In his book *Victory over Grumpiness, Irritation, and Anger*, Bible-based counselor and author Doug Britton writes about the importance of identifying anger patterns. He says, "The first step in overcoming anger usually is identifying what makes you mad." He includes a self-test in his book and at his website to help readers do this. As a way to start considering your anger, why not do this exercise from his website?

I get upset when...

____ I'm driving and someone cuts in front of me.

____ I'm driving and someone is a backseat driver.

____ I'm a passenger and someone drives too slowly.

____ I'm a passenger and someone takes a different route than I would.

____ I'm a passenger and someone gets lost.

____ I'm a passenger and someone parks in a different place than I would choose.

____ My spouse lets the car go down to empty.

____ My spouse doesn't load the dishwasher right.

____ My spouse criticizes the way I load the dishwasher.

____ My spouse weighs too much.

____ My spouse says I weigh too much.

____ My spouse is late getting ready for church.

____ My spouse comes home late.

____ My spouse spends too much money.

____ My spouse forgets something I said.

____ My spouse is clumsy or has an accident.

____ My spouse complains or worries.

____ My spouse or my children are noisy when I am trying to sleep.

___ My children are disrespectful.

___ My children fight.

___ My boss makes stupid decisions.

___ My boss gives me too much to do.

___ People are late.

___ Someone says mean words to me.

___ Someone takes advantage of me.

___ Someone ignores me.

___ Someone makes fun of me.

___ Someone accuses me falsely.

___ I think God treated me unfairly.

___ I think I do more than my share.

___ I am unappreciated.

___ Someone breaks a promise.

___ Someone lies to me.

___ Someone lies about me.

___ I walk into our home and it is messy.

___ We are out of milk or other items.

___ Our television breaks down.

___ My favorite sports team loses.

___ A politician does something wrong.

___ I don't like a sermon.

___ A pastor or board member ignores me.

Next comes this exercise.

When angry, I sometimes:

___ Yell.

___ Raise my voice.

___ Get irritated.

___ Am upset or grumpy.

___ Make sarcastic comments.

___ Put other people down.

___ Am impatient.

___ Withdraw or pout.

___ Feel bitter.

___ Feel resentful.

___ Feel sorry for myself.

___ Dwell on angry thoughts.

___ Other:[1]

Finally, Britton asks readers to estimate how many minutes they find themselves upset on an average day:

On average, I'm upset _____ minutes per day.

I hope you'll work through these self-evaluation exercises. You may discover some interesting patterns!

Trigger Points

Psychologists often speak of "trigger points" that lead up to anger. I've read that anger is not a primary emotion. Instead, it's a cover-up or alternative to the truth that our primary feelings may be too painful to talk about. Our real feelings are suppressed and hidden below the surface of anger. Over my 33 years of speaking and teaching, I've observed thousands of people. I've found that the appearance of anger can be a barrier to revealing the hidden secrets in our hearts. Anger camouflages low self-worth, jealousy, guilt, shame, fear, poor health, family secrets, personal secrets, alternative lifestyles, moral sins, bitterness toward God, grief over loss, financial issues, incest, regrets, misplaced priorities, negative thoughts, disappointments, and the list goes on and on.

One evening I was enjoying a wonderful dinner party in a lovely house in Small Town, Texas. The subject of anger became part of our conversation. A graceful, stately, pillar of the community said, "I hate Saturdays!"

I was stunned with her vehemence, and my jaw dropped. I finally asked, "What do you mean you hate Saturdays?"

"I'm *angry* on Saturdays. Why can't we just miss Saturdays? I hate that day of the week!"

My curiosity heightened, I asked her to tell me about Saturdays.

She said that when she was a girl her father abused her. He was the local pastor for the community, and on Sundays she had to sit and watch him preach as if nothing had happened the day before. Now an adult, every Saturday she sits at home, angry and afraid to go out because someone might hurt her if she leaves the safety of her secure living room. She's traumatized from her past and paralyzed about her future—and has been for more than 60 years. When she gets agitated or frustrated about something, especially on Saturdays, she's not just angry—she's trapped in her past with no hope for tomorrow. This is a sad state to be in.

In Your Own Words

❀ Do you think counseling would help this woman?

❀ Is she stuck without hope?

❀ Is feeling the way she does a sin? Explain your answer and support it with Scripture.

A Trigger Point Example

I discovered one of my trigger points of anger when I worked at a bank. A young lady who worked there had a habit of pointing her finger and shaking it in people's faces to get her point across. One Monday morning she got to work earlier than I did, and she discovered an error in the department where we worked. When I entered the area, she approached me about the error. Pointing her finger and waving it close to my face, she carried on and on.

I asked her to please stop and lower her finger so I could concentrate on fixing the error.

In response, she moved her finger even closer and got more adamant.

Angry, I reacted without thought. I caught her finger and twisted it. I didn't intend to hurt her, but I did. I was so sorry.

From that point on, both of us changed our methods of communicating. Thankfully I didn't get into trouble for my physical reaction. In fact, everybody she had pointed her finger at thanked me, including our boss.

I'm not advocating at all that this was the best way to deal with this situation. In fact, please don't handle your anger that way! It wasn't right. But I did realize that one of my trigger points is when people get pushy. (So please don't point your finger and wave it in my face. Thanks!)

In Your Own Words

❈ List some of your trigger points.

❈ How did you discover them?

❈ What are you doing to control them?

The Role of Stress in Anger

Unmanaged stress can lead to irritability, frustration, and outbursts of anger. According to one commonly used method for identifying stress and pinpointing key stressors, the top three stressful situations are:

- death of a spouse
- divorce
- marital separation

How can we eliminate the negative effects of anger and hostility in our lives? I have some suggestions:

- Learn to forgive others, and yourself. "To yourself be true."

- Don't be quick to take offense. Let negative things and words roll off you like water off a duck's back.

- Stay in an attitude of prayer all day. No, you don't have to walk around looking like an altar, but in your heart you can be ready and habitual to quickly and constantly lift up your circumstances and concerns to the Lord in the demands of the moment.

- Prepare your heart with praise music. You can sing and praise with your mouth or within your mind. God knows when you are sincerely praising Him. That's when you feel His loving presence rejoicing over you.

- Become familiar with the Holy Bible. Memorize verses so that when you don't have access to a Bible, you can go into your mental memory bank and recite what you need from your heart. I live by Philippians 4:6 NASB: "Be anxious for nothing, but in everything by prayer and supplication with thanksgiving let your requests be made known to God. And the peace of God, which surpasses all comprehension, will guard your hearts and your minds in Christ Jesus."

- Surround yourself with praying, positive-thinking people who will encourage, inspire, and empower you to do the right things.

- Tell yourself what my great-grandmomma often told me: "Two wrongs don't make a right, and it takes two to fight!"

Some angry people see their emotions in black or white. They're either raging mad or they're calm. They're on a cheerful high one minute and biting your head off the next. They're difficult to understand and get along with. Because most people experience some gradation of anger between the two extremes of rage and calm, the "black or white" extremists people tend to have difficulty recognizing when they're experiencing the intermediate anger stages. They don't catch the physical, emotional, and behavioral signs that let them know when they're becoming upset.

Here are some possible signs of anger one specialist identified:

Physical signs

- clenching your jaws or grinding your teeth
- headache
- stomachache
- increased and rapid heart rate
- sweating, especially your palms
- feeling hot in the neck/face
- shaking or trembling
- dizziness

Emotional signs. You may feel...

- like you want to get away from the situation
- irritated
- sad or depressed
- guilty
- resentful
- anxious
- like striking out verbally or physically

Also you may notice you are:

- rubbing your head
- cupping your fist with your other hand
- pacing
- getting sarcastic
- losing your sense of humor
- acting in an abusive or abrasive manner
- craving a drink, a smoke, or other substances that relax you

- raising your voice
- beginning to yell, scream, or cry[2]

Responding Poorly

As you can see, we tend to show our worst behavior when we're dealing with anger. Here are some helpful observations from Diane Eaton about our responses to anger:

> Anger tends to feel justified at the time and so does our response. We may reason, *She needs to learn a lesson or two. I'll show her!* So we assert ourselves over others by trying to manipulate and control them. After all, that is exactly what they have done to us. We reason, *Our offender deserves to be punished.*
>
> Anger that results from a threat to our security causes us to instinctively seek self-preservation. Perceived threats cause us to lash out in self-defense. While we are angry, our self-protective maneuvers feel justified, no matter how much damage they inflict on ourselves or on our offender.
>
> Our typical ways of responding to our anger can destroy us as well as fellow humans. In the long run, they do not produce restoration and peace of mind...
>
> Observation should lead us to conclude that, in general, we humans simply do not handle anger very well...It is because of our fallen human nature that our anger tends to produce ungodly responses.[3]

In Your Own Words

As you think about what the quoted specialists in this chapter have written regarding anger, respond to these questions.

❈ What are your "anger patterns"—the types of incidents that generate your anger?

❈ What are your "trigger points"—the situations or circumstances that typically lead to anger on your part?

❧ What are your "warning signs" that tell you you're getting angry or are angry?

❧ How capable are you at objectively recognizing these anger traits in yourself?

∾

I'm so glad I'm writing this book because I've discovered some things about me I've not really noticed before. There are some issues that push my buttons and rile me up. In fact, I believe these may be common trigger points for a lot of people.

- People who point their finger at me and wave it in my face.

- Hearing people complain about the same things all the time. I want them to get over it. Some things aren't worth rehearsing year after year, decade after decade.

- People who are never satisfied with me, no matter what I do for them. Everything in their lives is about them, and there's no room for anybody else's opinions or actions. If I say the sky is blue, they'll say it's red. I marvel that they don't get sick and tired of themselves sometimes. I say, "Give me a break and chill!" One of the greatest gifts we can give others, in my opinion, is the gift of gratitude wrapped in compliments. We can say, "Thank you so much. I appreciate you showing me that!"

I believe people's physical, emotional, and spiritual outlook would improve if we all avoided generating these trigger points for at least three consecutive weeks. Actually, it might just lead to good anger or righteous indignation!

Did I say *good* anger? Is anger ever good? We'll talk about that next.

> *Holy Spirit, please help me be fully aware of my trigger points*
> *so I can improve my response and not sin when anger rises.*
> *Help me to reflect You in every situation. Amen.*

3

Good Anger?

Once upon a time there were two different girls living in our home who had the same name. Well, almost. There was my daughter Lesa with an "e," and there was Lisa with an "i." We sometimes distinguished them when they were both with us by calling them "Little Lesa" and "Big Lisa." Let me explain.

My daughter Lesa told me one day that her friend Lisa was being put out of her home. I could hardly believe that. Lisa was 14 years of age. How could it be time for her to leave home? But Big Lisa was being told, apparently, that it was time for her to step out on her own and find a J-O-B. I was astounded.

My daughter was the same age as Lisa, and the two girls enjoyed the same activities. I told my daughter that if this news about her friend Lisa was true, "have her come home with you tomorrow after school, and we'll check with her father."

The next day when I went to pick up my daughter at the school bus stop, both Lesa and Lisa stepped off the bus together.

Well, that was some cause for concern. When we got home I called my husband. He came right home and telephoned Lisa's father. George asked, "Do you know where your daughter is?" And this father said, "No, I don't know where she is."

As they continued talking, Lisa's father said to George that he was sending Lisa out on her own. He confirmed that he'd said to her, "Listen, you're fourteen years old. You need to get out of the house and get a job. You don't need to get an education. When I was fourteen, I got out of the house and got a job, so you need to do that too."

Lisa was devastated. At this time her mother was in the hospital, and mother and daughter hadn't seen each other in a while. Lisa's father had married somebody else, and now she was being abandoned by her dad.

Needless to say, my husband experienced righteous indignation. He was so mad he hardly knew what to do. But he did the noble thing. George told this dad, "Listen, you come over here and give us the authority to be able to deal with her, and she can live here. When we eat, she will eat, and where we go, she will go."

You know, that kind of reminds me of the story of Ruth and her mother-in-law Naomi. Remember Ruth's beautiful words? "Where you go I will go, and where you lodge I will lodge. Your people shall be my people, and your God my God" (Ruth 1:16).

Anyway, we kept that girl in our home until she went to college. She is beautiful and intelligent. And she did well in college. After college she married, and now she has a very beautiful little girl, as well as a successful position in corporate America. She's doing quite well! Lisa and Lesa are still friends to this day. But I wonder where Lisa would have ended up if we hadn't agreed to keep her. Why am I sharing this story? I believe it shows that righteous indignation has a place in this world. We can be angry without sinning, and we can do the right thing in response to such righteous anger.

> *Thank You, Lord, for Your compassion and caring. And thank You for helping me reflect Your love by being sensitive to another person's need even in the face of inconvenience. Amen.*

Angry but Not Sinning

The concept of righteous anger or righteous indignation is one that comes to mind when we read Paul's words in Ephesians 4:26-27: "Be angry and do not sin; do not let the sun go down on your anger, and give no opportunity to the devil."

That's one of the most interesting and provocative passages in Scripture. In Matthew Henry's classic commentary on the Scriptures, he views the first part of this statement from Paul as a "concession… rather than as a command." Henry adds that *angry* is something "we are apt enough to be, God knows; but we find it difficult enough to observe the restriction, *and sin not.*" He further comments, "Though anger in itself is not sinful, yet there is the upmost danger of it becoming so if it be not carefully watched and speedily suppressed. And therefore, though anger may come into the bosom of a wise man, *it rests* only *in the bosom of fools.*"[1]

Here's how this verse is explained in a few contemporary study Bibles:

> Christians do not lose their emotions at conversion, but their emotions should be purified. Some anger is sinful, some is not…Satan can use our sins—especially those, like anger, that are against others—to bring about greater evil, such as divisions among Christians.[2]

> The Bible doesn't tell us we shouldn't feel angry, but it points out that it is important to handle our anger properly. If ventilated thoughtlessly, anger can hurt others and destroy relationships. If bottled up inside, it can cause us to become bitter and destroy us from within. Paul tells us to deal with our anger immediately in a way that builds relationships rather than destroying them. If we nurse our anger, we will give Satan an opportunity to divide us. Are you angry with someone right now? What can you do to resolve your differences? Don't let the day end before you begin to work on mending your relationship.[3]

> Not all anger is sin, but the believer should not be consumed by anger, nor should one's anger even be carried over into the next day, as this will only give an opportunity to the devil.[4]

In Your Own Words

- After seeing the comments on Ephesians 4:26-27, look at that passage in your Bible again. What do you believe you are being taught?

- How might this passage relate to the concept of righteous anger or righteous indignation?

Jesus Got Angry Too

Do you remember our discussion about Adam and Eve and their punishment after sinning in the garden of Eden? Did God kill them or wish them ill? Did He take all their talents and skills from them and beat them up? Did God continue to bring up their sin, causing them continual shame? Did He taunt them, yell at them, separate the two of them? No! God allowed the consequences of their disobedience to take place while giving them another chance at life. Our God is an *awesome* God! He loves us even when we do wrong. He always gives us another chance. Glory to His name!

How common is righteous, appropriate anger in our lives? Is it something we should encourage and develop? We need look no further than the life and ministry of our Savior Jesus Christ to see a biblical portrayal of righteous anger. So let's dive into the Word of God.

In the Gospel of Mark we see an occasion where Jesus is specifically said to be angry. And it is an anger mixed with grief:

> Again [Jesus] entered the synagogue, and a man was there with a withered hand. And they watched Jesus, to see whether he would heal him on the Sabbath, so that they might accuse him. And he said to the man with the withered hand, "Come here." And he said to them, "Is it lawful on the Sabbath to do good or to do harm, to save life or to kill?" But they were silent. And he looked around at them *with anger,* grieved at their hardness of heart, and said to the man, "Stretch out your hand." He stretched it out, and his hand was restored. The Pharisees went out

and immediately held counsel with the Herodians against
him, how to destroy him (Mark 3:1-6).

In Your Own Words

❀ What made Jesus angry in this situation?

❀ Think about the heart condition of those Jesus was angry with. Is
this similar to the heart condition of many people today? If so, who
are those people? Do you believe we should be angry with them?

⌀

Sometimes Bible teachers say that Jesus' anger was also on display
when He cleared out the temple. (He apparently did this twice—early
in His ministry, as recorded in John 2, and near the end of His ministry, as recorded in Matthew 21, Mark 11, and Luke 19.) *Anger* and
wrath aren't used in these passages, but the word *zeal* is. As you look
over the following two descriptions of these events, think about what
might have been going on in Jesus' heart.

> The Passover of the Jews was at hand, and Jesus went up to
> Jerusalem. In the temple he found those who were selling
> oxen and sheep and pigeons, and the money-changers sit-
> ting there. And making a whip of cords, he drove them all
> out of the temple, with the sheep and oxen. And he poured
> out the coins of the money-changers and overturned their
> tables. And he told those who sold the pigeons, "Take
> these things away; do not make my Father's house a house
> of trade." His disciples remembered that it was written,
> *"Zeal* for your house will consume me" (John 2:13-17).
>
> Jesus entered the temple and drove out all who sold
> and bought in the temple, and he overturned the tables
> of the money-changers and the seats of those who sold
> pigeons. He said to them, "It is written, 'My house shall

be called a house of prayer,' but you make it a den of rob-
bers" (Matthew 21:12-17).

In Your Own Words

✷ Why do you think Jesus did what He did?

✷ Do you think they are cases of righteous indignation? Why or why not?

✷ What indications do you see that Jesus was in full control of His emotions?

✷ What do you learn in these passages that might help you better understand anger?

Jesus' Anger and Our Anger

I think Diane Eaton offers some healthy things to think about as we compare our anger with the anger of Jesus:

> Jesus experienced many anger-producing situations in his life. He was frequently mocked, assaulted, and attacked. There is not one reference to him being angry and reacting with vengeance, retaliation, or self-protection. On the contrary, his willingness to submit himself to crucifixion revealed that he did not resist evil by attacking the offenders with an angry response. Instead, he resisted the real enemy—Satan—by dying on the cross.
>
> People are quick to use Jesus' temple experience as an example to justify their anger responses. However, he was not vengeful, he did not control, and he did not cause damage to anyone. His response was not punitive or to retaliate. On the contrary, he was at the temple to offer mercy and forgiveness. He always wanted to see people restored to God rather than condemned.

Jesus did not avoid "making people angry." In fact, many times Jesus said or did something that deliberately produced an anger response. No wonder that he didn't survive long. Anger soon bore its evil fruit. One day a mob of people angrily shook their fists shouting "Crucify him!" just as Psalm 2:2 prophesied, "The peoples plot in vain... against the LORD and against his Anointed One."

Jesus was right when he said that anger was like murder (Matthew 5:21-22). He himself was the victim of human anger. We must ask the question: couldn't Jesus have tried to avoid so many anger responses by wording his thoughts differently, or by doing his "offensive" miracles away from the Jewish leaders? Why did he deliberately arouse anger in people? Was this loving?

I believe that Jesus did this to give the people a chance to ask themselves the question, "Why am I angry?" He gave them an opportunity to discover what was at the core of their hearts. If they had admitted their anger, they could have admitted their sins and their need for his mercy, and that could have restored them to God. Sadly most of them refused to admit their anger, and they refused to examine their heart. Instead, they vented their fury at God and scapegoated his Son, including his followers. That is still happening today.[5]

Evaluating Our "Good" Anger

After seeing that Jesus was angry at times, we might be tempted to give ourselves lots of freedom to be angry. On the other hand, we need to be careful when it comes to this powerful emotion.

Most of the time, our anger *is not righteous*. We make excuses for being mad at people by blaming them for our conduct. God's Word warns us about being angry at people because of what they say or do. The fruit of the Spirit listed in Galatians 5:22-23 includes self-control. We are charged to exercise this trait.

It's true there are anger-causing situations that sometimes need to be brought to the surface by talking through them and dealing with the significant issues that are dangerous or combustible. But there is really never a time when we should lose our cool or retaliate. As James wrote, "Human anger does not produce the righteousness that God desires" (James 1:20 NIV).

By giving in to anger, we're often staying focused on our interests and opinions. Instead, we should be equally concerned about other people's concerns and welfare.

The Bible says God doesn't want us to simply react emotionally to others' actions. No! He wants us to act wisely and with a gentle spirit. We're told to conduct our lives "with all humility and gentleness, with patience, bearing with one another in love" (Ephesians 4:2) and respond "in the meekness of wisdom" (James 3:13). Yes, that's right. Wisdom and gentleness are God's solutions for dealing with people who may not be as open to His goodness, grace, and mercy as we are.

And do you know that the words *righteous indignation* are not found in the Bible? Reflect again on Ephesians 4:26: "*Be angry* and do not sin; do not let the sun go down on your anger." So, is there such a thing as good anger? Sure is!

When you feel anger rising, ask: Would God be angry in this situation? Why would He be angry? Is that what I'm angry about?

The wisdom-laden book of Proverbs tells us,

> There are six things the LORD hates,
>   seven that are detestable to him:
>   haughty eyes,
>   a lying tongue,
>   hands that shed innocent blood,
>   a heart that devises wicked schemes,
>   feet that are quick to rush into evil,
>   a false witness who pours out lies
>   and a person who stirs up dissension in the
>   community (6:16-19 NIV).

If your anger is centered on these or similar issues, such as idolatry, disobedience to God, and other sins, then you're probably in the ball game.

But if you're fighting back at people and trying to get even, you're sinning. Anger—your anger and my anger—can easily flow into sin. You know that person who pushes your buttons? Be careful. Instead of falling back on your response history, you can break the chain and relieve your panic by giving the situation to God and calling on Him for guidance.

I recall being a speaker in the state of Georgia. I was standing on the platform when the Spirit of God whispered in my mind. He said, "You're praying wrong." I thought, *What is going on here? What am I hearing?* The impression I received was very clear: "When you pray for someone, you're praying wrong. Pray against the spirits harassing that person. 'We do not wrestle against flesh and blood, but against principalities, against powers, against the rulers of the darkness of this age, against spiritual hosts of wickedness in the heavenly places.' It's not the person who is acting on his or her own; it's the spirits that are acting against them."

This was a life-changing moment in my life. I remembered this idea was taught in Ephesians 6:12 so I added it to my arsenal for attaining victory over anger. If we are going to be angry and not sin, we must know who is against us so we can fight the battle effectively.

In my book *Don't Give In...God Wants You to Win!* I listed some ways the demons harass us. These are the schemes of the devil that he uses to try "to steal, and to kill, and to destroy" (John 10:10). Satan's goals are to...

- destroy our faith
- demoralize us
- redefine the battle
- bring division among us
- deceive us
- lead us into error
- gain influence over us

- prevent conversion to Christianity

- dilute our Christian efforts

The devil uses all these schemes to tear us down and strip us of our hope for something better. By reacting angrily to someone's conduct, we fall into the sin trap Satan sets up against us. This trap leads us in the wrong direction—taking us down the low road of ungodly thoughts and behaviors instead of climbing up to God's standards. The low road is where selfishness, blame, disgust, fights, brawls, accusations, intimidation, frustration, agitation, bickering, slander, and other negative reactions live.

Frankly, I've chosen to take the high road in spite of how rocky it can get. On the long journey of life, the high road assures us of more peace, contentment, gentleness, patience, tolerance, and temperance. It ain't easy, baby, but it's sure worth it!

Carnal Anger vs. Righteous Indignation

In my research on anger, I've read that there is *carnal anger* and there is *holy indignation*. The word *carnal* suggests people thinking more about themselves and how things affect them than they think of others. Their concentration is controlled by their flesh, the appetites and passions of their bodies and minds. They seek sensual pleasures and immediate gratification rather than spiritual good. This focus is human, temporal, worldly, and secular.

An example of carnal-minded anger is Cain in the Old Testament of the Bible. He killed his brother Abel because he was jealous. God had accepted Abel's offering but not his. Cain wanted the attention his brother got, not realizing that Abel was appreciated by God because of his obedience and humility. Abel's heart was pure; Cain's wasn't. And Cain became bitter and angry.

Vindictive actions are carnal actions and are, therefore, sin. Carnal minds can take offense at anything at any time. Sometimes I think carnal people thrive on being mad at someone and creating strife. And the people they're often mad at or jealous of are often those who live for the Lord.

God's anger, however, is *always* in accord with holiness. His anger is righteous indignation. He doesn't take action to punish or retaliate. You can be sure that God's motives are always honorable and for our benefit.

Righteous vs. Self-righteous Indignation

When we think about righteous indignation, we often look back at the times when Jesus was upset. Remember that Sabbath day when He reached out to heal a man with a withered hand? The Pharisees were ready to pounce on Him for "doing work" on the holy day. The Bible tells us that Jesus "looked around at them *with anger*, grieved at their hardness of heart" (Mark 3:5). Jesus was angry as well when He cleared the temple of the money-changers twice.

One Bible teacher elaborates on this and then wisely contrasts it with something we need to watch out for:

> Righteous indignation is a justifiable contempt and loathing of a situation or a behavior that is just not right... When we see a disregard for the standards of God's law on matters such as sexuality, abortion, or justice or the complete breakdown, it seems, of an ethical standard in the financial industry, it is perfectly legitimate to experience indignation, a distaste and even anger, over such things...
>
> On the other hand, there is also what might be called, not a righteous indignation, but a *self-righteous indignation*. Self-righteous indignation does not arise out of seeing something that is completely at odds with God's holy law, a righteous motive, but rather it arises from making *yourself* the standard of righteousness...
>
> Self-righteousness feels so good! It is so good when we can put others down to make ourselves look good. It feels so good to do like the scribes, and put our man-made rules and piety and sensibilities above the needs of others. It feels so good to do like the Pharisees, and look down upon all the "sinners" around us, to experience that exhilaration, that rush, of self-righteous indignation...

But when you think about it, it's pretty sick, isn't it, to build yourself up, by tearing others down?

Now is the time to repent. Now is the day of the Lord. The kingdom of heaven has drawn near. Jesus said: "Those who are well have no need of a physician, but those who are sick...For I came to call not the righteous, but sinners." He came for you and me. And thanks be to God! Amen.[6]

In Your Own Words

❀ Summarize the distinctions between anger that is good and righteous and appropriate and anger that is wrong.

❀ Why is it so important to have an accurate understanding of these distinctions?

4

Angry at God?

Here's a story a friend sent to share with you in this book.

After a long illness accompanied by much hope and many prayers for his healing, my dad died. As a 14-year-old daddy's girl, I was devastated. My mom became a basket case, crying herself to sleep at night and sleepwalking through the day. We found ourselves deep in debt, with no income, and about to lose what little we had. The four of us children, ages six to fifteen, all got odd jobs to pay the bills and pretty much had to fend for ourselves.

I think I was numb for a year or so, and then I became resentful. I was angry toward God for not answering my prayers, for taking my dad and leaving us like this.

My heart stayed hard and cold toward God until my early twenties. By this time I had put myself through college, gotten married to a fabulous guy, and had a wonderful job. Yet my life felt flat and empty.

Then a charismatic Christian woman, whose husband was a seminary student, came into my life. We worked every day together, and she was always talking about God and inviting me to her church. I found this annoying and aggravating, but due to her genuine kindness and persistence, we became friends. I knew she was praying for me, as was my mother who had since recovered from her grief.

Then one day the poem *Footprints* came across my desk. It was as though I heard God say to me, "I never abandoned you, child; I carried you through. I have watched over you, wept over you, and blessed you!" I looked at my life, and the truth of this struck me. The fact that despite the odds, I not only survived, but thrived, and that although I had let go of God, He had never let go of me.

That day I rededicated my life to the Lord. I released the anger that had tormented me and stolen my joy during the previous years. My life went from being gray and one-dimensional to Technicolor 3-D! Praise the Lord! He has truly come to seek and save the lost and to set the captives free. I am a testament to that!

From what I can tell, this woman's experience of being angry at God is something a great many people share.

In Your Own Words

❈ Is anger toward God something you've experienced? If so, what brought this about?

Going Broke

I've allowed myself to become angry with my circumstances and rail at God. In the mid-1980s I was enjoying a very prosperous time. My business was flourishing, and so were my husband's. We didn't have a major care in the world. One person even told me she was jealous because God seemed to be so much better to us than He was to her. All was well in our lives. I was traveling all over the world writing management programs for corporations and implementing them. This was the perfect world.

Life suddenly changed. Banks failed in two Southern states, and that greatly affected the financial status of many of us who worked and invested in the financial arena.

Within six weeks I lost all my scheduled speaking dates. For several months my arrogance kept me from worrying. Then I noticed our declining bank balances. George's businesses were hurting as well. I got my head out of the sand and stopped assuming the phone was going to ring any minute and a million-dollar contract would be awarded to me...or that a several-million-dollar check presentation would come to my door. It hit me: *We're going to be broke if something positive doesn't happen soon.*

Our checkbook balance kept falling, my husband's businesses were failing, the phone was not ringing, my marketing plan wasn't successful, and we were wading in a sea of bills and money owed. This was a new situation for us, and we didn't know how to handle it. My husband got sick from worry and embarrassment because he lost two once-successful businesses. Soon we were drowning in an ocean of debt. I got miffed with God. I railed at Him as I asked if what the Bible taught was really true. As people who tithed and gave regularly, I expected to see obvious fulfillments of God's promises to watch over us and care for us—in the manner I wanted Him to, of course. But I didn't see any prosperity being manifested or hinted at.

Six years passed before I experienced real victory over this anger. While driving one day, I saw a bumper sticker that read: "Life is tough and then you die!" I bought into that until I drove further and saw another bumper sticker that announced: "Tough times don't last; tough people do." Those words altered my life forever.

I started singing and praising God for what I had: gas in the car, food to eat, a house to live in, and utilities paid. I had health and strength, wonderful children, good friends, and mostly *hope*. I surrendered my feeling of lack to the God of plenty. Before long He revealed a major financial breakthrough that proved to George and me that He had been and was still in charge of our finances. He had not abandoned us. *Hallelujah!* We learned to never give up on the goodness of the Lord and that we could count on Him to keep His promises.

Anger, rage, railing, distrust, and lack of faith perpetuate carnality. But we can defeat that worldliness by believing God's Word, holding on to hope in Jesus, and being tenderhearted and kind to the people around us. Yes, those people may not understand us, and they may rub us the wrong way so we feel our anger rising. But we can respond in a godly manner. It may be hard to achieve, but we can succeed by asking God for wisdom and strength.

Rage Against God

The book of Job revolves around a wealthy man who experienced great trials and setbacks. In fact, he lost everything he had, including his children. As Job was aching and crying out in his misery, one of his counselors and friends asked him, "Why has your heart carried you away, and why do your eyes flash, so that you vent your rage against God and pour out such words from your mouth?" (See Job 15:12-13 NIV.)

One commentary I read on this passage asked, "Is it wrong to be angry with God?" Then the author answered the question this way:

> No. The problem comes when legitimate feelings of anger are not handled correctly and lead to inappropriate bitterness and rebellion which sometimes accompany anger. The Bible realistically portrays the frustration and anger of God's people when things go wrong or when they cannot understand why certain things happen. This was the reason for Job's anger. Not only did he feel he was being treated unjustly by God, but he could get no explanation from him.
>
> Jonah's anger over Nineveh's repentance and over the death of the shade-giving vine was inappropriate (Jonah 4). Twice the Lord questioned him, *Have you any right to be angry?* (Jonah 4:4,9). The prophet Jeremiah grew angry with God because of his persecution and the lack of response to his preaching. But he went too far when he accused God of lying (Jeremiah 15:18). Immediately, God told him to repent and stop uttering foolish words (15:19).

Ultimately, that is where Job ended up. Though his suffering caused many questions and anguish, he went too far when he insisted that he had a right to an explanation. In the end, God spoke to Job and set him straight: God had the right to question Job, not the other way around (38:1-3). Job realized he had been arrogant and that his anger was unjustified. When confronted by the awesomeness of God, Job repented (42:6).[1]

A Complex Question

Is it *ever* right to be angry at God? John Piper deals with this question in the kind of thoroughly biblical, carefully reasoned, passionate way he's known for. He compares that question with another one: "Is it right to *express* anger at God?" He says, "These are not the same question, and the answer is not always the same." To get a bigger picture, he considers what it really means to be angry with somebody. "Anger at a person," he notes, "always implies strong disapproval. If you are angry at me, you think I have done something I should not have done. This is why being angry at God is never right. It is wrong—always wrong—to disapprove of God for what he does and permits."

So if we feel angry toward God, should we try to stuff that feeling and basically become hypocrites by pretending it isn't there? Piper says no: "If we feel it, we should confess it to God. He knows it anyway. He sees our hearts. If anger at God is in our heart, we may as well tell him so, and then tell him we are sorry, and ask him to help us put it away by faith in his goodness and wisdom."[2]

Normal to Be There, but Not the Place to Stay

Similarly, Bible-based counselor and author Doug Britton asks this tough question: "Is it a sin to be angry with God?" He summarizes his answer with these words: "It's normal to sometimes feel anger at God. Just don't stay there." Britton also notes:

Have you ever gotten angry with God when you or someone you love goes through hard times? If so, you aren't alone. In fact, many people get angry with God from time to time.

People who get mad at God often feel guilty about their anger and think their anger makes God angry with them. Their guilt sometimes drives them into feeling condemned or distant from God…

One thing I appreciate about God is that I can be real with him. If I am angry with God, I can be honest about it instead of thinking I must hide it or act "religious." I know this by reading in the Psalms about times when David openly expressed anger or frustration with God.

Although it's a normal thing to do, it's a shame when we get angry with God, for he is our best friend. Yet since we are people, it happens.

What's both interesting and encouraging to me is that almost every time David expressed complaints toward God, he ended up praising God. That's a good resolution to our anger. (Notice that in verses 1-6 of Psalm 22, David voices his complaint. Yet in verses 22-31, he praises God.)

It's just the same with our (human) friends. We get angry with them at times, yet in the end we turn back to them since we love them and we know they love us.

I'm not saying it's a good thing to get angry with God. When I do, I am showing how little I understand his love, his goodness, and his purpose. I need to face my anger and deal with it, as David did.

Plus, the better I know God, and the longer I walk with him, the less likely I am to be angry with him. But, if I do get angry, I am glad he understands and helps me come to a place of repentance.[3]

Let's take a moment to pray about this.

Lord, help me refrain from being angry with You for my circumstances. Please give me the wisdom and knowledge to understand that from the uncomfortable situations You allow, You bring about good. You are truly my light and my salvation! I have nothing to fear in You. Thanks, Jesus. In Your name. Amen.

Look at His Hands

For anyone who's ever felt angry toward God, here is heart-stirring, mind-stimulating counsel from Randy Alcorn:

> When we feel upset with God and tempted to blame him, we should look at the outstretched arms of Jesus and focus on his wounds, not ours.
>
> When we lock our eyes on our cancer, arthritis, fibromyalgia, diabetes, or disability, self-pity and bitterness can creep in. When we spend our days rehearsing the tragic death of a loved one, we will interpret all life through the darkness of our suffering. How much better when we focus upon Jesus!
>
> "Let us fix our eyes on Jesus...who for the joy set before him endured the cross." The following verse commands us, "Consider him who endured such opposition from sinful men, so that you will not grow weary and lose heart" (Hebrews 12:2-3).
>
> However great our suffering, his was far greater. If you feel angry at God, what price would you have him pay for his failure to do more for people facing suffering and evil? Would you inflict capital punishment on him? You're too late. No matter how bitter we feel toward God, could any of us come up with a punishment worse than what God chose to inflict upon himself?...
>
> If you know Jesus, then the hand holding yours bears the calluses of a carpenter who worked with wood and carried a cross for you. When he opens his hand, you see the gnarled flesh of the nail scars on his wrists. And when you think he doesn't understand your pain, realize that you don't understand the extent of his pain. Love him or not, he has proven he loves you.[4]

In Your Own Words

❅ What do you think about being angry at God now?

❅ If you're ever inclined in the future to become angry with God, what do you want to remember most from this chapter?

5

Anger and Our Children

Oh my goodness! I've never noticed so much anger and rage in children as I'm seeing with my grandchildren. I'm also seeing it a lot in some of their friends. Lord, have mercy on us.

At one time I met reguarly with some teenaged girls in my church. They're all grown-up now with positions and homes of their own, but years ago they asked me to mentor them. I'd overheard one teen say to another, "These people need to stay out of my business and leave me alone!" This aroused my curiosity so I asked what she was talking about. She replied, "These old people act like we don't have sense, and they're always trying to tell us how to dress and act. I'm tired of it, and the next time she says anything to me, I'm going to tell her off."

My suggestion to her was to have a sleepover at my house so I could find out what was going on between this girl and the lady she was speaking about. I hoped that if I could meet with the young girl and her friends informally, they would tell me what I needed to know to make a judgment regarding the situation. Then I could help ease the conflict.

The young girls came to the sleepover, and they taught me so much. I discovered that they had overheard this lady talk about other people in an accusatory fashion, and they were offended by what they had heard. Their anger wasn't because of a direct confrontation, but an offense because of hearsay. I believe this happens a lot in schools too. After that first meeting they asked if we could meet often to discuss life. I agreed and benefited so much during our times together.

Too many children feel victimized because of hostility in their homes, separation from parents and other loved ones, seeing or being a victim of brutality, and becoming latchkey kids left alone without supervision. Statistics indicate there are three million children abused in America each year! And 80 percent of people 21 years old reported abuse in their childhoods. Can you believe it? It's so sad. Meanwhile, bullies—boys and girls—are significant problems in schools.

Children not only need discipline and correction, they want them. When they don't get constructive discipline, they think nobody cares about them. They feel estranged. When they're not included in group or family activities, they long for that affiliation. When they have nobody their age to communicate with, they feel left out. Getting passed over in class or outdoor activities and not doing well in school sometimes stirs them to misbehave to receive attention—and any kind of attention will do. The more they do this, the more people point them out, and the more hostile everyone becomes. And when teens are caught doing things they know are wrong, they can get angry at themselves and cause even more problems.

It's our precious responsibility and privilege to be parents and grandparents and mentors to kids. And we especially want to gain a solid understanding of anger—our anger as we deal with the challenges of interacting with young people and the anger that arises in the children—so we can help them.

Personality Differences

Back when one of my daughters was 12 years old, I had really had it with her. Here's why. When we would go out, I'd introduce Vikki to people I knew, yet she was so nonchalant and uninterested it was embarrassing. I believed she didn't like people very much. She preferred to stay in her room where she could read or do whatever she wanted. She was just not very social. But she still needed to learn social skills!

When we met someone she would say, "Hi." And that was it. End of conversation. And she said it very indifferently, as if implying, "I really don't care about meeting you."

Well, I was embarrassed because she acted rude and I thought she was being disrespectful of my friends and me. I got so sick and tired of her doing this. One day I had a nervous breakdown about it. I got so angry, so upset, so fed up with her! I said, "Vikki! When I take you out and introduce you to people, I want you to open your mouth and act like you have had some home training. *Smile* at them and *be courteous* to them. Stop being so antisocial!"

But you know what? That didn't faze her a bit. Not one little bit. In fact, she folded her arms, looked dead-straight at me, and replied, "Momma, I'm not you. I don't want to be like you."

"What did you say!" I demanded. You can guess that I got very defensive about her comment. Not only did I want to hurt her because she refused to mind me, but she went on to insult me by saying she didn't want to be like me! I accepted and interpreted her words as "I don't like you, and I don't want to be anything like you."

I stayed upset about that for a long time. In fact, although I knew I had to feed her, I didn't want to have anything to do with her. I was really mad about her attitude. I didn't even want to look at her. I was *really* mad. To top it off, here I'd been thinking I was a Proverbs 31 woman and all my children would rise up and adore me and want to be like me. Oh my!

But after I got over being insulted—and I admit it wasn't just two or three days. Honey, I stayed angry with Vikki for a *long* while! Finally, I started really thinking about what she'd said. *Hmmm. She's not me, and she doesn't want to be like me. So what's* wrong *with me?* But from there I moved on and wondered, *Maybe there isn't anything wrong with me. Maybe it's just her personality.*

So I began to become objective about that. And as I did and considered what she said, I realized that what she was really telling me was "I'm not you, Mom. I can't be like you. God made me who I am. Please accept me the way I am." And so I got over the irritation. It took me a while, but I got over it. And I started respecting her personality, which really is so different from mine. I also began to see the traits that were her strengths and the many unique features God had created in her.

So I've learned that this is another type of situation that can cause us to get angry—when we have expectations of people that they can't or don't want to meet, that are unreasonable, or that reflect who we want them to be. We want people to value what we do and want to imitate us, yet everyone is unique. People are treasures in their special ways. I'd been upset with Vikki because I expected her to be this outgoing, extroverted socialite like I am. But that's just not how God made her.

Very often when our anger seethes it's because we are looking for someone to act and be and do like us. We compare other people to ourselves, especially if we are happy with who we are and think we're handling life just fine. Kids especially seem to suffer from comparisons to other people. I believe this is one of the things that causes them to become so angry. Often they're negatively compared to their parents, or their sisters, or their brothers, or their relatives of similar ages, or to other children in school. I've heard people say (and, yes, I've even said it), "Why can't you be like so-and-so?" Well, God didn't make him or her like so-and-so. And when I hear that statement now I think, *Why do we so often try to make people over into our own images?*

This is a real problem children face. If there's a child in the family who excels in what we think children should excel in, and another child is not doing as well in that area, we'll say to that second one, "See what your sister did? See what your brother did? Why can't you make grades like that? Why can't you act like that? Why don't you want to be in sports like they do?" All those comparisons! And I'm sure when children hear them at home or at school or at play it creates a feeling of inferiority in them. They feel like they're not as good as anyone else.

And this holds true for grownups too! We're often negatively compared to others in our workplaces, our homes, our finances, and our recreation pursuits. Adverse comparisons create bouts of anger, shame, and disgust. They can even spark the desire for retaliation.

Something else that creates anger in children and adults—but especially children—is when someone shows favoritism. When a parent favors one child over another, it can very easily create anger, frustration, and a sense of not measuring up. An example of this is when a parent buys one child something, but doesn't get another child something that is comparable. And if a parent spends more time with one child than the other, it sends a message that the excluded one interprets as, *I'm not worth enough for Mom to spend time with me. She doesn't like me.* And that leads to anger and acting out behavior.

Here for Me?

Let me share a story.

When my youngest daughter, Lesa, was 14, I was away from home quite a lot. I was a member on various boards of companies and the meetings and activities required a lot of time. I was also working at a bank during the day and teaching banking practices in the evenings. I was away from home every day of the week doing something for somebody.

That year Lesa was excelling in school. She was very excited about making the school's drill team. I remember very well one day when I was starting out the door for another busy day. Lesa—this meek, mild, tender, loving child—came up to me and looked me straight in the eye. She said, "Are you ever going to be here for anything I'm doing?"

Ouch! That stuck a dagger into my heart. I hadn't intentionally abandoned her, but I had essentially done just that. I'd been rationalizing that George was there for everything so there was no harm in me missing many of her activities. I was thinking, *I can still be part of th urban league, and the Dallas bank chamber, and go to church all the tin and travel and teach, and do whatever I'm doing. I can be busy like th every day of the week, and it's okay if I don't spend a lot of time with Le*

Well, here she was on the drill team, and I hadn't really taken t time to watch her perform. I was so into me—so self-centered. N Corporate America, Mrs. Trying-to-make-a-name-for-myself. I forgotten the foundational formula for raising a child. Thank the I my child was feeling very secure in herself—secure enough to cal onto the carpet! She surely was.

And when I looked into her sad eyes, I replied, "Yes, honey, be here for what you're doing."

That's when I started reevaluating my life. I realized, *I'm in all of these groups and all of these important meetings and I'm prominent in the community—but my child is suffering from my inattention.* I thank God she said something to me! Thank God she reached out for my attention.

I looked at all the organizations that I was a part of, and I asked, "Are they doing me any good? Am I doing them any good? Why am I really doing this?"

I'm sure you're smart enough to figure out why I was doing so much. I was doing it because I was trying to make a name for myself instead of raising my youngest child. I was leaving her alone with her dad while I was going out and trying to be Mrs. Whosever-will, Mrs. igh Society, Mrs. Big Thing, and Mrs. All-that-and-a-bag-of-chips. And so I had planted seeds of disappointment and hurt and anger in daughter—and even seeds of fear. All because of my self-centeredness. , I stopped a lot of what I was doing. I resigned from almost every- I was in. I recouped my relationship with my daughter—and today he best of friends.

g Our Children Control Anger

gnizing the various ways that we experience anger can be a in raising children who handle anger well. In his book *How Love Your Angry Child,* Dr. Ross Campbell emphasizes the e of home atmosphere in helping children effectively han-

parent I know cares deeply about the emotional pment and maturity of his or her children. They know that, when the time comes for them to leave they will be succeeded by warm, caring, conscien- cessful, and well-loved sons and daughters.

hen anger rages out of control in a family, that ly isn't possible. Children are incredibly sensi- motions of their parents. They cannot live in usehold without bearing the imprint of that le incident of mismanaged anger will cause forgettable pain, and a pattern of it will do permanent damage. On the other hand, mature handling of anger is a powerful force that will intensify the love between parent and child.[1]

In his article "Teaching Kids to Control Anger," Christian author Ron Rhodes emphasizes the importance of "lowering the emotional temperature of your home"—making it less tense and more loving. He shares these important points:

1. Teach your children simple coping techniques—such as taking a deep breath and counting to ten. Some cool-down time spent in one's room can also be extremely beneficial as a means of avoiding rash actions or words.

2. Allow and encourage your children to verbally express their anger to you in a calm way. Children must be allowed to express why they feel the way they do, even if it involves pointing a finger toward you (and, yes, there will be occasions when they're right about something you did wrong). If allowed to give verbal expression to their anger, kids will be less likely to give physical expression to their anger.

3. Of course, you must be careful not to allow your child to cross the boundary into disrespect. Verbal expressions are allowed, but verbal assaults are off-limits.

4. Keep the lines of communication open and talk a lot. Your children need to know that mom and dad are always there with an open ear. If they feel like you never listen, their temperature will definitely rise on the anger barometer.[2]

Calming Them Down

In her book *Parents Do Make a Difference: How to Raise Kids wit Solid Character, Strong Minds, and Caring Hearts,* Dr. Michele Bor directs our attention to six specific ways to help children handle an I think you'll find her suggestions constructive and encouraging.

These ideas have been presented to hundreds of parents in my workshops and the feedback has been positive. They're simple techniques, and when used consistently they will work...

1. Model calmness. The best way to teach kids how to deal with anger constructively is by showing them through your example! After all, you don't learn how to calm down by reading about it in a book, but by seeing someone do it. So use those frustrating experiences as "on-the-spot lessons" to your child of ways to calm down...

2. Exit and calm down. One of the toughest parts of parenting is when children address their anger towards us. If you're not careful, you find their anger fueling emotions in you that you never realized were in you. Beware: anger is contagious. It's best to make a rule in your home from the start: "In this house we solve problems when we're calm and in control." And then consistently reinforce the rule...

3. Develop a feeling vocabulary. Many kids display anger because they simply don't know how to express their frustrations any other way. Kicking, screaming, swearing, hitting or throwing things may be the only way they know how to show their feelings. Asking this kid to "tell me how you feel" is unrealistic, because he may not have learned the words to tell you how he is feeling!...

4. Create a calm-down poster. There are dozens of ways to help kids calm down when they first start to get angry. Unfortunately, many kids have never been given the opportunity to think of those other possibilities. And so they keep getting into trouble because only behavior they know is inappropriate ways express their anger. So talk with your child about acceptable "replacer" behaviors.

You might want to make a big poster listing them. Here are a few ideas a group of fourth graders thought of: walk away; think of a peaceful place; run a lap; listen to music; hit a pillow; shoot baskets; draw pictures; talk to someone; sing a song...

5. Develop an awareness of early warning signs. Explain to your child that we all have little signs that warn us when we're getting angry. We should listen to them because they can help us stay out of trouble.

Next, help your child recognize what specific warning signs she may have that tell her she's starting to get upset such as, "I talk louder, my cheeks get flushed, I clench my fists, my heart pounds, my mouth gets dry and I breathe faster." Once she's aware of them, start pointing them out to her whenever she first starts to get frustrated. "Looks like you're starting to get out of control." Or, "Your hands are in a fist now. Do you feel yourself starting to get angry?"...

6. Teach anger control strategies. A very effective strategy for helping kids to calm down is called "3 + 10." You might want to print the formula on large pieces of paper and hang them all around your house. Then tell the child how to use the formula: "As soon as you feel your body sending you a warning sign that says you're losing control, do two things. First, take three deep slow breaths from your tummy." (Model this with your child. Show her how to take a deep breath then tell her to pretend she's riding an escalator. Start at the bottom step and as you take the breath, ride up the escalator slowly. Hold it! Now ride slowly down the escalator releasing your breath steadily at the same time.) "That's 3. Now count slowly to ten inside your head. That's 10. Put them all together, its 3 + 10, and it helps you calm down."[3]

In Your Own Words

❀ What have you learned in this chapter that will be of the greatest benefit to you in helping your children deal effectively with anger?

❀ What do you believe the results will be if you teach your kids how to manage anger well? Be specific.

∽

> *Father, You understand all about caring for Your children—including me! Help me to be more like You as I raise or mentor children. Give me understanding, appropriate discipline guidance, wisdom for avoiding favoritism, ideas for creating peaceful environments, and godly wisdom to teach my kids and those I encounter about You and how to handle anger in ways that honor You. In Jesus' name. Amen.*

6

Anger Management

Anger management is a popular concept. It includes a great many techniques and approaches advocated by countless specialists, counselors, managers, and seminar trainers. Although simple response techniques don't have the capability of rooting out anger in the way that God's power can, I do believe there are helpful and constructive techniques we can learn and put into practice that will help us approach and handle anger more calmly and objectively.

Get It All Out

If you are feeling a strong sense of bottled-up anger, the first thing I encourage you to do is *talk with somebody* about it. Emotionally and mentally this is a healthy thing for you to do. *Everybody* needs somebody to confide in. Yes, honey, I said *everybody*. We also need someone who will listen to our questions and concerns and respond in a helpful manner.

For this to really work, make sure the person you choose to meet with is capable of giving you *godly wisdom*. You know, someone who loves God and is constantly learning more about Him. Don't go to just anybody. Almost everybody will offer an opinion, but opinions not based on God's truths can be wrong. Opinions can also be hurtful, fault-finding, and confusing. So when you choose somebody to talk to, make sure she reads God's Word regularly. Find someone will share God's teachings in a wise way to help you make decisions. Let it be someone who will pray with you and help you find answers for yourself in the Bible.

Anger can lead to depression and other negative conditions when we try to keep that strong emotion suppressed or ignore it. The objective is not to get all emotional and rant and rave and carry on. Be reasonable, stay as calm as possible, stick to the current situation, and share your heart. So whoever and whatever you're angry about, you need to *do* something about it. What you *don't* need is to keep holding it inside where it can fester.

Here's another suggestion. Get a pen or pencil and a piece of paper. Sit down and write a letter to the person(s) you're angry at. Even if he or she is not alive anymore write the letter.

Say *everything—yes, everything!*—that's on your mind, including the ugly stuff, the stupid stuff, the surprising stuff, the scary stuff. Get all the hatred, the malice, the frustration, the disappointment out in writing.

After some time has passed for you to mull over what you've written, evaluate how you're feeling. If you sense the anger is still there, well then, write another letter. You can keep writing letters as long as you feel angry or upset. You may need a legal pad and lots of pens or pencils. Whatever it takes, get your anger out.

Now pay special attention to the next instruction: *DO NOT* *MAIL that letter! DO NOT MAIL any of the letters.* Put them in a safe place until you've achieved victory over your anger and the situation. *DESTROY* them. Do not keep them around.

Now, maybe you don't want to write down any of this. Maybe you think you're not good at expressing yourself in writing. Another idea is to "talk to a chair." Put a paper bag on the chair to represent the people you're angry with. And then start talking. Tell them what you think and feel. Don't go on a tirade, but share your feelings.

Make sure you're alone...that nobody's listening or might accidentally hear you. This is a private conversation. (After all, if we told everyone what we think about them, we wouldn't have any friends, because no one is perfect, and everyone experiences problems in

The main point is to find some way of getting the poisonous anger out of your system. This will help the healing process begin.

In Your Own Words

🔖 I encourage you to take a moment and write down your plan for talking through your anger, whether it's conversing with a real person, writing letters you won't mail, or visualizing a conversation with the people you're having trouble with. Be as brief or detailed about this plan as you want to be, but put something down in writing. This will help you be committed to following through and motivate you to make it happen.

Anger-Management Techniques

Here's a list of common anger-management techniques:

- *Count to 100:* When people are angry they can say or do things that they regret later. If you feel you are becoming angry, do something to cool down, such as counting to 100, and then continue the discussion later.

- *Leave the room:* If the situation is getting to the stage where people are yelling or are possibly even being violent, *tell them you will talk about it when they and/or you are calm* and then *leave the room.*

- *Write down your feelings:* Like writing poems? Songs? Or just writing? Great—get some of that anger out using your pen. Write down all your frustrations—this way it doesn't hurt anyone.

- *Exercise:* Do something active like kicking a Hacky Sack, riding a bike, or going for a run. This will give you a chance to release some of the energy and calm down a bit.

- *Play video games:* If you feel as if you are going to get into a fight, it's better to do so while playing a video game rather than doing it in real life. This might be a good way to release some anger and energy.

- *Play some tunes:* Strap on the headphones and play your favorite tunes for a while.

- *Sit in a quiet place:* Go to a park or wherever you feel calm and just chill out. After you feel calmer (have counted to 100 or played some calming music), think about why you are angry and come up with some solutions to the problem you are having. It may be that you need to talk to someone because you can't work it out yourself. This is pretty common. A lot of people can't work out the real reason why they get so angry.

- *Talk to a counselor:* There are lots of counselors out there who are available to listen and help you work through your anger. There are even counselors who specialize in anger-management techniques—learning about these can help you heaps. You can find counselors at your school or local community health center.[1]

In Your Own Words

⚘ What anger-management techniques from the list will you try the next time the need arises?

7

More Help for Controlling Anger

Here's another story sent to me from a friend to share with you. It's a good illustration of how a change in mindset can make a huge difference in controlling our anger.

From Negative to Positive

My father was perfectionistic with an explosive temper, so it should have come as no surprise that, although I swore it would never happen, when my children were small I began to follow in that pattern. My oldest child was extremely strong-willed and defiant, and as a young mom I felt so weary and worn down that it seemed I had little resistance to the moment-by-moment challenges she presented me with. If I told her, "No, don't touch," she would look squarely into my eyes and plant her little finger right on it, just to show me that I was not calling the shots. No matter what the topic, if I said hot, she said cold.

Every day turned into a determination that this would be a better day. A chipper "hello" before long turned into the first, the second, the third, and the fourth clash of wills. Then I would explode. I would find myself screaming hurtful things, tossing her onto the sofa, and having to leave the room to flee her sobs. This was the course of events—sometimes numerous times a day.

I lived in a miserable, depressed state of defeat and guilt. I had always dreamed of being a mom, and I loved children, but no matter how hard I determined in my own strength to change, reformation eluded me.

One morning, after tearfully seeking the Lord, He led me to scriptures that spoke of the power of the tongue, the necessity of my coming under submission to Him, allowing the Holy Spirit to empower me, and of the fact that love, peace, and self-control were fruit of the Holy Spirit. I was convicted to speak His life into this situation, to speak the positive by faith. As soon as I felt any frustration, I was to call on Him for help.

I began to avoid saying things like "you drive me crazy" to my daughter, instead telling her, "You are such a blessing!" I would make positive pronouncements from the get-go: "You are a wonderful girl who makes her mommy so happy." I found that she became less and less defiant, and I had more grace with her and more patience in general. The explosions of anger became fewer and further apart, until they became a rarity.

God is so good, and there is indeed power in the spoken Word! Today that daughter, as well as my other three children, are beautiful, happy teenagers who do not struggle with the curse of my father's Irish temper I inherited. Praise the Lord! I thank the Lord that through the wisdom of His Word and the power of the Holy Spirit, I became the mom God intended for me to be, and that now my children have risen up and call me blessed!

Looking for Hope

For some people, anger is extremely intense and all-consuming. Not long ago I started something I call Project HOPE. The very first thing I did was to go to some rehabilitation centers in our city where the homeless and the prostitutes go.

On one particular day I went to a homeless shelter that serves 8000 people every month. I met with the men and the women who wanted to come and were allowed to come to the meeting we held. The shelter was really something to see and experience. The homeless were of all ages—children, teenagers, on up to older men and women. I could see anger in many of their eyes—as well as disappointment, and embarrassment, and, yes, some loneliness too.

The evening of the same day, I went to a rehab house that reached out to prostitutes. There was one lady there who, from the moment I walked in the door and saw her, I could tell she had problems. Analyzing her on the basis of how she appeared, she would come across as haughty and not very likable. But I knew there was something deeper inside her that would tell a different story and convey a different impression.

When she came in, she seemed to be trying to appear really first-class. At first I thought she was a rehab employee rather than one of the residents. Later, as we got into the mentoring session, I noted that her face was contorted. She was very upset. She was crying—not with any outward sobs, but the kind of crying that is so silent yet so real that I could cut it with a knife. Tears were running down her face. But as we got further into the teaching, she acted like she wasn't listening, like she didn't want to be bothered. It seemed that nothing we were saying was hitting home with her.

Only later did I find out this was her disguise. You see, in her past she had been abused, she had been belittled, she had been accused, and she had been set aside. A lot of bad things had happened in her life. And she was particularly angry because she had a broken relationship with her mother. She said her mother cared more about money than she did about her.

This woman was also angry because a man who had been a strong and loving figure in her life—she never told us whether this man was her father or someone else—had died, and she said he had been the only person who really understood her and who cared anything about her. She was also angry because, she reported, her children were estranged from her.

Now, I didn't know any of the circumstances about her. I had no idea of those things. But I did know that she was so angry she didn't want to hear what anybody had to say. She was mad at God, and I suppose she was mad at herself. She was angry about all the circumstances she had been in. And she showed it. She was belligerent; she was unkind; she was almost nasty.

But I looked at her with a heart of compassion because I knew that the mental prison she was living in gave her continual frustration. She was living in a jailhouse without bars that was eating her up. She was a victim who saw no way of release or victory.

Well, we talked with her. There were a number of other people in the room—enough to serve together as a helping presence, but not so many as to overwhelm or alienate her. Many of the people attending felt some of the same things she did, but I don't think anyone there was as mad as she was. As we sat and talked with her, she started spilling out things. It was almost like she was throwing up these things because she was in a place where she knew no one would hurt her. She was aware of this security, and it allowed her to release the things she just had to get out—all the vice, and the venom, and the vulgarity.

She spoke about how she wanted some relational skills. She wanted to know how she could get her mother to pay attention to her, to love her. And how could she get people to not judge her for her past. And how could she help her children understand what was going on with her.

I didn't know the circumstances that got her on the street, but by looking at her I could tell she'd grown up in a good family. She apparently had a good education; she was very astute, very learned. And yet here she was in such distress and trouble.

Of course, even a stable and healthy background isn't a guarantee that people will make wise decisions. In difficult circumstances some people choose to go down a destructive path. But I thank God that circumstances can also be overcome with His help. And that the situations surrounding what God is doing will free us from having to remain in the states of anger and distress we find ourselves in at times.

As we talked with this woman, I eventually saw a glimmer of light in her eyes…a glimmer of hope. It was swiftly passing, but I believe I recognized that certain thoughts had entered her mind: *Maybe God isn't as bad as I thought He was. Maybe I need to take a closer look at this.*

We listened, and we embraced her. We loved her without expecting anything in return. We spoke to her about how loving God is. We encouraged her to read her Bible, especially starting in the Gospel of John. And we held hands and prayed with her and over her. I'm trusting God that this will prove to be a help to her.

After this particular session that evening, there was a play given by my daughter for the ladies in the rehab house, and this woman came to see it. It was such a true-to-life play that depicted a lot of the situations the ladies were going through. I pray that it offered another glimmer of help to them all—and in particular the angry woman I spoke with.

I thank God that He gave me the privilege and opportunity that evening of watching some people work through their issues, through their trials, through their tribulations, and I look forward to seeing what the end results may be. I've not gone back to that rehab center yet, but I will be going in a few days. I'm anxious to see if what we discussed and learned a little more about helped the women hold on to hope.

Is Anger Controllable?

Can we really control our anger? The following perspective taken from the Yahshua Institute website may help us answer that question:

> All of us do control our tempers, when it is important enough to do so. Consider a mother who has a terrible day. The washer leaks on the floor, kids fight, supper burns, she breaks her favorite bowl, kids track mud on her clean floor. So she explodes, screams at the kids and threatens them. Then the phone rings and it's her husband's boss. Suddenly she is quite capable of carrying on a polite conversation.
>
> Dad works on the car. The dealer gives him a wrong part, it won't go together right, then it won't run, and a wrench slips and splits his knuckle. He's screaming and using profanity. Then a car pulls in the driveway; it's the preacher's wife come for a visit. Suddenly he is calm and polite.
>
> We can control our anger, when we really want to. If we can control our temper for the sake of other people, why not do it for God? God sees everything we do. Is God important enough to control our anger for?[1]

We all get angry, but the fact is that anger can work for us or against us. Why don't we commit to becoming aware of our fears, faithlessness, insecurity, displaced expectations, and the truth about our relationship with God? As I tell my grandchildren, we are not responsible for how people treat us; we are responsible only for our responses to them. Nobody has command of our thought patterns but us. And nobody is responsible for our mental and emotional well-being but us.

Each of us is a threefold person made up of the body, soul, and spirit, and all three need to line up with each other before we can experience wholeness. When the mind (soul) is angry, the body is sick and the spirit is troubled. That's a signal that something is out of sync that perhaps we can't fix.

I believe that only the Person of Jesus Christ, through His redemptive blood, is able to put us back together again as whole human beings who have the spiritual tools to live calm, peaceful, and contented lives. We must completely surrender our imperfections and sins to the Lord, telling Him all about our struggles, acknowledging that we are sinners, and asking Him into our hearts. Praise God, He will forgive us and spiritually come to live in our hearts. He will forgive us and restore us to lives of redemption and salvation.

Only when we give ourselves to the Lord will we be in sync to master our anger. The forgiveness of Christ and His coming to live inside us is the proof that we're restored and able to be reconciled to our brothers and sisters.

When we say, "All to Jesus I surrender—my anger, bitterness, and strife. I will depend on Him to help me resolve my anger issues with myself, my friends, my family, and any others," then we'll be in harmony—body, soul, and spirit working together to make even the foulest clean.

The Key to Dealing with Anger

Here's a good summary I found of how to deal with our anger by getting it to work *for* us rather than against us:

> Anger is a powerful force. And this world contains many angry people. It's not just nonbelievers who experience anger and who vent their rage. Even Christians struggle with the

powerful forces of anger. Anger is a rampant problem that wrecks families, harms children, tears apart churches, and divides the body of Christ. Are you an angry person?

Most people can probably identify times in their life in which they have been angry. Others can identify those things that really tick them off. We all have our areas and we all have our pet ways of responding to angry circumstances. But how do we deal with anger?

Dealing with anger doesn't take a simple step-by-step formula. It's not realistic to think that Christians can undergo some kind of behavior modification to get rid of sin. There is only one antidote to sin. It is the gospel. It is the good news that you're a sinner, God loved you, and Jesus came to earth to take the penalty for sin that you deserve. It's the good news that by accepting His sacrifice for you, you can be forgiven and live a new life for Jesus.[2]

A Racing, Red Fire Truck

Yes, there is indeed a remedy for any fire of anger that burns within us. I'm reminded of when those bright-red fire trucks come racing up to put out a fire. They come in a hurry, don't they? They come with their hoses and pumps ready to spray water. And when one of those hoses is turned on and that beautiful water comes gushing out, that liquid puts out the fire—and even covers the embers so that they will not catch fire again.

From God's Word we know there is water of cleansing in the river of life—water that can make the foulest clean. That's what Jesus did. The blood that came out when He was pierced in His side—His blood is a purifying stream that can extinguish the fires of the anger and hatred that live in this world.

That red fire truck symbolizes the blood of Jesus to me. And to all who are saturated with the fire of anger, Jesus says, "This is My blood, the blood I shed on Calvary's cross so you never have to be destructively angry again." No, we don't have to be captives to sin and anger.

Oh yes, be angry at the things that are not right in this world, at the sins and injustices. But don't sin and create greater havoc because of your anger. As Christians, we are to have a distaste for worldliness. We steer away from vulgarity, drunkenness, sexual promiscuity, and all things we know are displeasing to God. But although we have a distaste for those things, we should never feel hatred or condemnation against the people who are caught up in those activities. Hate the sin but not the sinner. If we allow hatred, its fire burns us and may sear the hearts of those who desperately need to see the love of Jesus shining through us.

God made every human being. He knows all about each one of us. Toward those whose ways are not in accordance with His, who have not come to the point in their hearts of trusting Him, we are not to be judge and jury. We are to take them the good news that Jesus came so they can be made clean and filled with life. All the dirt in their lives, all the anger and venom, all the poison that is in them will be eliminated through Christ.

So when the consuming fire of anger threatens to ignite and blaze within our hearts, we've got the water from the river of forgiveness standing by. We've got the blood of Jesus that was shed for us ready to cover the situation.

In recognition of that, we've got to open our mouths and tell people about Jesus. After all, if we were getting physically burned, we would scream for help, wouldn't we? So what do we scream when we want to escape the fires of anger? *"Jesus! Jesus! Jesus!"*

What else will we do? We'll call out to God! "God, forgive me! Help me! God, please clean me up!"

Oh yes! And as soon as we call on Him, He is quicker to respond than a bat of our eyelids. He's there to take away the poison and quench the fire of anger that smolders within us.

Friend, I know this is true! I've experienced it! I encourage you to talk to God. Ask Him to cleanse your heart and soul and life. He'll do it because He loves you. That's His will—and He wants to perform His will in you.

The Aftermath

Now, there may be scars that remain after you're burned even though the fire is out. But the places that were burned, once they're healed, will become stronger and stronger. And you'll be able to help someone else put out his or her fires of anger and hatred.

I once had second-degree burns on my arm, and the skin there is still scarred. But I seldom even notice it's there anymore, and I don't feel the excruciating pain the burn caused. I do remember putting salve on it and how much it soothed my skin.

Now when you have a burn injury, you wash and clean off that burn—clean it out and make sure it stays clean. Because if it doesn't stay clean, it might get infected. We don't want an infection; we want healing. And you cover that burn with a healing, soothing salve, and then you make sure it's wrapped and protected so no more dirt can get in it.

That's what needs to happen with our souls that have been burned by anger's fire. They have to be washed in the cleansing blood of Jesus and cooled by His living water. And we've got to put on a salve. This is the Spirit's soothing, healing power. As an African-American spiritual says, "There is a balm in Gilead to heal the sin sick soul." And we need to wrap that wound with the Word of God and tape it up with prayer so no dirt or debris can make its way back in.

And when that wound from anger is finally healed, the scar may be there but we won't dwell on it or consider it because it's healed.

Baby, do you really want to be healed of the anger that burns within you? From the vengeance that boils? From the hatred that spews? From the trauma that keeps you down? If so, look up to Jesus, the author and the finisher of your faith. The first thing you should do is ask Him for forgiveness. And then He will surely help you forgive others because He heals *you* and He forgives *you*. As soon as you ask for His help—oh, my goodness!—He forgives. He does not hold any grudges against you.

Oh, I know there are some people who teach that God is mean or vindictive. That He is always angry and ready to strike someone down if he or she doesn't do the right thing. But, honey, read the New Testament in your Bible—the new covenant God made with us. You'll discover He doesn't work that way. The New Testament is filled with stories and truth about a wonderful gift called *grace*. (One day I'm going to write a book about that!)

Jesus gives you grace. The apostle Paul writes, "There is therefore now no condemnation for those who are in Christ Jesus" (Romans 8:1). *No condemnation! None!* When you ask for God's forgiveness, and then you forgive the sins of others—the hurts against you and any disappointments caused by others—then God says to you, "Forgiven!"

And when you are forgiven, you are released from the debt of sin. So why not help release other people from their debt? Forgive them and show them how God will set them free too.

In Your Own Words

❆ Do you believe your anger can be effectively controlled? Why or why not?

❆ What have you learned in this chapter that is most helpful for dealing with your anger?

8

Anger's Harmful Effects

One of the most vile, heinous, unpredictable, and crazy things in life is to build up anger and hatred so much that we don't really realize what we're doing to ourselves and the people around us. I say this based on a situation where the consequences of anger cascaded until lives were ruined. The primary person involved had no idea what was going on inside her because of her choices. Her choices reveal that she is filled with rage and anger and torment, and those poisons have devastated her life and affected the people around her.

Genita's Story

I will call this particular young person Genita. Yes, that's a good name. Genita was in a relationship, but it went sour. I guess neither person realized why, judging by how they dealt with the responsibility for it.

At the time, Genita was on drugs and drinking alcohol. She was lying and cheating and scheming and manipulating to get what she wanted. I imagine that being under the influence of things like that she wasn't fully aware of what she was doing. Those things grab people so much they lose sight of what's going on and why. I think this is what happened to Genita.

Genita put her cash in the hands of this person she was in a relationship with. He deceived her about the money and spent it.

Now Genita had entered this relationship at much too young an age. This relationship didn't work, so when they split up, Genita was bitter and angry. Yep, she was all that and more.

Then she entered another relationship. And she took all of her anger baggage into her new relationship because nothing had been resolved from the previous situation. Perhaps Genita didn't even know what was going on inside her. She was living and acting on all the resentment, hatred, agony, distrust.

Genita's anger caused her to become the abuser in her new relationship. And when she did that—well, all kinds of things erupted, including physical fighting, pulling knives and weapons, tearing up the partner's clothes, lying, stealing, and more. Oh, it was a mess.

She also got into trouble with the law. In fact, she got into so much trouble that she was in and out of court-ordered rehabilitation and law-enforcement facilities more than 15 times.

Now, she'd had a relationship with someone else before she went to jail the first time. While she was gone, that person moved on to a relationship with somebody else. Genita decided that she was going to come back and make that relationship work. But because of all the enmity that had built up inside her over the years, she couldn't bridge the gap and make it work. She lost that relationship again.

Then she got into another relationship, and this person really did care for her. He was doing his very best for her and trying to help her. But Genita kept damaging this relationship because she had all that stuff built up in her, all that baggage of distrust.

I believe she didn't like herself because she was so disappointed in herself. You see, Genita came from a great family. She was exposed to the best things in life. She had the promise of a wonderful life and career. And then, when she turned 17, she started drinking. And that led to the use of drugs and all the other schemes that so often accompany that kind of life. She even went into a psychiatric hospital a couple of times. The doctors said she'd developed some kind of malfunction of the mind.

Genita never got to the root of her anger. I don't know what the exact root of her anger was—maybe something happened in her childhood, maybe she was abused. I don't know. But I do know that she kept hanging on to all that evil and its poison.

She finally lost that latest relationship, and now she's mad because all those relationships failed. She continues to be irritable and tense and bitter. She doesn't know how to converse with anybody. When I'm around her I feel like I have to walk on eggshells. She's always putting other people down, but she never sees what she's doing.

That's what anger will do when it's bottled up in a person. It's a poison that kills the soul. And on our own strength, there's no antidote for it. With the Lord's help we can let it out, deal with it, and watch it dissipate. We've got to pray it out, and we've got to trust Jesus.

I know Genita has praying parents. She has praying siblings, and she has praying grandparents. But nothing as yet seems to be breaking through Genita's barriers. She knows who God is; she knows how she was brought up. Remember the scripture that says, "Train up a child in the way he should go; even when he is old he will not depart from it" (Proverbs 22:6)? I believe what that passage is saying is, "Give that child the training he or she should have—the biblical training, the ethical training—and that child will never forget what he or she has been taught about God, even if they persist (at least for a while) in rejecting it."

Maybe the child will never turn back. Oh, my goodness. That *is* a choice every person makes. Some people live amid the disasters and torment of their own activities so much they become angry with themselves as well as with God. They don't realize how much anger builds up and contributes to their lives' downward spiral. And there is much that must be done in their hearts—much that we must pray for—to bring them to a fresh recognition and a final acceptance of the biblical truths they were once taught.

Self-hatred is so all-consuming! I look at Genita and I think, *God, why don't You just jerk her back to You? Put her in a place where she absolutely must listen to You?* And you know, I think God does that sometimes because that's His will for our lives—that we pay attention to Him.

And when we're open to that, He will speak to us in many, many situations. He speaks to us, but so often we fail to listen. We don't listen because, first, we don't want to. Second, we're afraid of doing what He might tell us to do because the unknown is scary.

I've talked with Genita. I've talked to her about her relationship with God. And what she says is, "I don't feel about Him the way you do. I don't think about this the way you do. I think it's all a setup."

That cop-out allows Genita to stay upset with herself and angry with the world. She created and is perpetuating that world! She chooses to be angry and see everything around her through eyes of anger, bitterness, and distrust.

And now the angry life she inhabits has led to a number of physical complications that have compounded. She has liver problems; she has heart problems; she has sleeping problems. On top of those, she has mental problems.

And she continues to have relationship problems that will never cease until she views herself the way God sees her...until she accepts the fact that there truly is help for her in her anger, that there is hope for her in Jesus. Until she grasps that and is willing to become as humble and as meek as a lamb to receive the goodness that God has for us all, she'll continue to suffer.

Oh, my! How many people live in states of trauma and travail because they are trying to be their own gods, their own saviors?

I hope you fully recognize that anger is self-centeredness. Anger is debilitating. And anger is keeping so many people down, keeping them from experiencing the joys of life. For, you see, joy comes when we know who can solve our problems!

Anger's Impact on Health

Genita's health problems reinforce for me the conclusion that many medical and other specialists are reaching more and more: Anger is bad for our health. Here's one summary of what's being discovered in current research:

> It is important to understand what happens to the body when one becomes angry. In a moment of anger, you may experience muscle tension, grinding of teeth and teeth clenching, ringing in the ears, flushing, higher blood pressure, chest pains, excessive sweating, chills, severe headaches or migraines.

With chronic anger people can also experience peptic ulcers, constipation, diarrhea, intestinal cramping, hiccups, chronic indigestion, heart attacks, strokes, kidney problems, obesity, and frequent colds. Medical experts have found the heart muscle is affected by anger, and anger can actually reduce the heart's ability to properly pump blood.

The results of prolonged anger can harm the body's largest organ, the skin. People who hold in their anger often have skin diseases such as rashes, hives, warts, eczema and acne. Researchers have studied the relationship of anger and skin disorders and discovered that when a person resolves his anger, skin disorders dramatically improve.

One of the major effects anger has on the body is the release of chemicals and hormones, primarily the adrenaline and non-adrenaline. The adrenaline hormones act on all organs that reach the sympathetic nervous system, stimulating the heart, dilating the coronary vessels, constricting blood vessels in the intestines, and shutting off digestion.

Suppressed anger can also have psychological effects, causing depression, eating disorders, addictions to drug and alcohol, nightmares, insomnia, self-destructive behaviors, and can cause disruptions in the way a person relates to others.[1]

Learning to better control anger may well be one of the best things we can do for our overall health.

Protect Your Heart

A recent article at WebMD focuses on how frequent high levels of anger have been linked to heart disease:

So how exactly does anger contribute to heart disease? Scientists don't know for sure, but anger might produce direct physiological effects on the heart and arteries. Emotions such as anger and hostility quickly activate the "fight or flight response," in which stress hormones, including adrenaline and cortisol, speed up your heart rate and breathing and give you a burst of energy. Blood pressure also rises as your blood vessels constrict...

"You get high cortisol and high adrenaline levels and that is the cardiotoxic effect of anger expression," says Jerry Kiffer, MA, a heart–brain researcher at the Cleveland Clinic's Psychological Testing Center. "It causes wear and tear on the heart and cardiovascular system." Frequent anger may speed up the process of atherosclerosis, in which fatty plaques build up in arteries, Kiffer says. The heart pumps harder, blood vessels constrict, blood pressure surges, and there are higher levels of glucose in the blood and more fat globules in the blood vessels. All this, scientists believe, can cause damage to artery walls...

Some doctors now consider anger a heart disease risk factor that can be modified, just as people can lower their cholesterol or blood pressure.[2]

An angry heart is a heart that's unwell.

In Your Own Words

❁ What have you learned in this chapter that's helpful for you in facing up to your anger?

❁ In what ways might you be currently experiencing physical effects from anger?

∞

Gracious Healer, I know there are physical effects of anger that cause bad health. Please help me pinpoint any areas of my life that are being adversely affected by anger. Give me wisdom for dealing with them. Help me get on the right track so I won't go against Your will. Thank You, Lord! Amen.

Part 2

Looking Closer:
Anger in God's Word

9

What God's Word Teaches About Anger

In our journey together through this book so far, we've heard stories of people encountering anger, and we've heard observations about anger from a wide variety of specialists and teachers. Along the way, we've also looked at a number of scriptures about anger. Now, for the rest of our journey, we're going to intensify our focus on God's Word and truths.

Anger's Tragedy for Two Brothers

One of the early instances of anger we find in Scripture leads to terrible tragedy for the first two children born into this world. Those two children, of course, were the boys Cain and Abel, the two oldest sons of Adam and Eve. Let's review how their tragedy began. It begins when these two boys had grown old enough to go to work.

> Now Abel was a keeper of sheep, and Cain a worker of the ground. In the course of time Cain brought to the LORD an offering of the fruit of the ground, and Abel also brought of the firstborn of his flock and of their fat portions. And the LORD had regard for Abel and his offering, but for Cain and his offering he had no regard. So *Cain was very angry*, and his face fell (Genesis 4:2-5).

There's probably a great many details we'd like to know about this that we simply aren't told. But one thing for sure is clear: Cain is very angry.

In Your Own Words

❧ What do you think this passage might be telling you about Cain and his relationship with God?

❧ Did you notice how Cain's anger was immediately and physically apparent? How does anger usually catch your attention?

⊘

Cain's anger certainly got God's attention, not that He needed any clues, of course. God saw right into Cain's heart. Notice how He responds to Cain in his condition:

> The LORD said to Cain, "Why are you angry, and why has your face fallen? If you do well, will you not be accepted? And if you do not do well, sin is crouching at the door. Its desire is for you, but you must rule over it" (Genesis 4:6-7).

That opening question God spoke to Cain is actually a simple one, isn't it? "Why, Cain? Why are you being this way? What's the real reason for it?" I wonder if God wants us to understand that when we're angry, the first thing we need to grab hold of in our minds and hearts is a clear understanding of the reason for it. Exactly what are we angry about? And then we need to calm down for a moment and objectively take a look at and recognize what's happening.

Did you note how quickly God warns Cain about the terrible danger of his anger and what it can lead to?

In Your Own Words

❧ Restate God's warning to Cain in your own words.

❧ How do you think this warning relates to you in your times of anger?

⌒

In Cain's situation, we know how terribly correct God's warning was. The very next verse tells us: "Cain spoke to Abel his brother. And when they were in the field, Cain rose up against his brother Abel and killed him" (Genesis 4:8).

There are other scriptures that further explain what was happening with Cain and Abel. First John 3:12 helps us answer the "why" question about Cain's anger and the crime it led to: "We should not be like Cain, who was of the evil one and murdered his brother. And why did he murder him? Because his own deeds were evil and his brother's righteous." Contrast this picture of Cain with what we read about Abel in the New Testament: "By faith Abel offered to God a more acceptable sacrifice than Cain, through which he was commended as righteous, God commending him by accepting his gifts. And through his faith, though he died, he still speaks" (Hebrews 11:4).

In Your Own Words

❧ Looking at the two New Testament verses just cited, what seems to be the most significant difference between Cain and Abel?

❧ How do you think that difference might relate to how you need to respond to anger?

❧ Based on what we've discussed so far, at the time Cain first experienced anger, how should he have dealt with it?

❧ What could Cain have done to avoid being so consumed by his anger to the point of committing murder?

⌒

Cain was punished for his crime. God sentenced him to a lifetime of being "a fugitive and a wanderer on the earth" (Genesis 4:12). The Bible even tells us that "Cain went away from the presence of the LORD" (verse 16). What a sad and awful picture.

Now imagine you are one of Cain's parents (Adam or Eve). Reflect on what had happened to your oldest two sons and what it might mean for you and your remaining offspring.

In Your Own Words

❧ What important lessons about anger and dealing with anger do you draw from this situation?

❧ Going back to that first question God asked the angry Cain, answer it for yourself: "Why are you angry?"

❧ Think about the types of situations that make you angry. What are the most common causes of your anger?

❧ What further understanding does the story of Cain and his anger give you regarding the reasons for your anger?

❧ What questions, if any, does the Cain and Abel story raise in your mind about anger?

Anger's Danger

We can see in God's Word that even when anger is understandable and permissible, it can still lead to reactions that are very wrong. For instance, among the biblical patriarch Jacob's 12 sons, two of them—Simeon and Levi—seemed particularly prone to violent anger. Note how strongly Jacob speaks about this:

> Simeon and Levi are brothers; weapons of violence are their
> swords…For *in their anger* they killed men, and in their

willfulness they hamstrung oxen. *Cursed be their anger, for it is fierce, and their wrath, for it is cruel!* I will divide them in Jacob and scatter them in Israel (Genesis 49:5-7).

In Your Own Words

❊ What significance do you see in the words and imagery associated with anger in these three verses in Genesis 49?

❊ Jacob also says, "Let me not enter their council, let me not join their assembly" (49:6 NIV). Why do you think Jacob wanted to distance himself from his sons?

∞

The barbarous actions done by his sons that Jacob refers to were explained in Genesis, chapter 34. There we read the sad story of how Jacob's daughter, Dinah, was abducted and sexually assaulted by a Canaanite man named Shechem. Shechem then wanted to keep Dinah as his wife. Because of the abduction and rape, Dinah's brothers Simeon and Levi took vengeance by killing every male in the city where Shechem lived (verse 25).

Lawrence Richards points out in his expository dictionary:

> The anger of Simeon and Levi…was justifiable. But their action—tricking and murdering all the men in the rapist's city—is "sternly condemned" by their father's words in Genesis 49. Even justifiable anger does not justify any sinful actions that the anger may stimulate.[1]

We've got to be careful about where we let anger lead us. We can't let it control us.

In Your Own Words

❊ In this situation regarding Simeon and Levi, how might they have responded differently in dealing with their anger so they wouldn't be subject to such a harsh judgment from their father?

℅

Proverbs 27:4 says, "Wrath is cruel, anger is overwhelming." In our hearts, anger can become like a controlling tyrant that affects everything about us.

Angry Times

In the book of Exodus, we see the Egyptian Pharaoh and Moses provoking each other to anger. At one point, Moses and Aaron "were driven out from Pharaoh's presence" (10:11). And later, according to verse 28, "Pharaoh said to [Moses], 'Get away from me; take care never to see my face again, for on the day you see my face you shall die.'"

Moses wasn't immune to anger. He "went out from Pharaoh *in hot anger*" after he announced the last and worst plague God would bring on Egypt—the killing of all Egypt's firstborn males (see Exodus 11:4-8).

This "hot anger" that Moses demonstrated is quite interesting when we remember that "the man Moses was very meek, more than all people who were on the face of the earth" (Numbers 12:3). Moses was not an arrogant, short-fused person who constantly got steamed about something. But as he repeatedly witnessed the hardness of Pharaoh's heart, he found something to be angry about.

In Your Own Words

⚘ How would you explain this anger of Moses to someone?

⚘ Is this an example of righteous anger? Explain.

℅

The English Standard Version Study Bible offers this possible explanation for Moses' anger: "As the one who has interacted with Pharaoh throughout and even pleaded with the Lord on his behalf, it may be that Moses found Pharaoh's persistent pride infuriating because of the devastating effect it would have on the people of Egypt."[2]

But surely the anger of Moses in this instance was also an expression of God's feelings. There's no doubt God was angry with the Pharaoh and the Egyptians. In Psalm 78:43-51 we read a summary of what the Lord did to them during this time: "[The Lord] let loose on them *his burning anger, wrath, indignation, and distress,* a company of destroying angels. *He made a path for his anger;* he did not spare them from death, but gave their lives over to the plague."

We can also learn in this particular situation a thing or two about how to rightly respond to the anger of others. Hebrews 11:27 tells us, "By faith [Moses] left Egypt, *not being afraid of the anger of the king,* for he endured as seeing him who is invisible." Moses wasn't afraid of Pharaoh's anger because Moses had his eyes and heart fixed on "him who is invisible," the mighty God in heaven.

In Your Own Words

🌺 What do you think Moses understood about God's character that helped him not be intimidated by Pharaoh's anger?

🌺 What can you remember about God's character that will help you not be intimidated by the anger of others?

More New Testament Teachings on Anger

Jesus linked anger with murder in these sobering words spoken in His Sermon on the Mount:

> You have heard that it was said to those of old, "You shall not murder; and whoever murders will be liable to judgment." But I say to you that *everyone who is angry with his brother* will be liable to judgment; whoever insults his brother will be liable to the council; and whoever says, "You fool!" will be liable to the hell of fire (Matthew 5:21-22).

In Your Own Words

☙ What does this reveal about Christ's attitude and perspective regarding anger?

⊂⊃

Let's look at some other key New Testament passages that teach very directly about anger. Consider each one carefully and ask God to show you how it applies to your situation.

In Your Own Words

☙ How does this verse relate to your anger? "Be angry and do not sin; do not let the sun go down on your anger" (Ephesians 4:26).

☙ How does this verse relate to your anger? "Let all bitterness and *wrath and anger* and clamor and slander be put away from you, along with all malice" (Ephesians 4:31).

☙ How does this verse relate to your anger? "Now you must put them all away: *anger, wrath,* malice, slander, and obscene talk from your mouth" (Colossians 3:8).

☙ How about this one? Does your anger lead you sometimes to want to "pay somebody back"? "Beloved, never avenge yourselves, but leave it to the wrath of God, for it is written, 'Vengeance is mine, I will repay, says the Lord'" (Romans 12:19).

☙ Once more, how does this verse relate to your anger? "I desire then that in every place the men should pray, lifting holy hands *without anger* or quarreling" (1 Timothy 2:8).

☙ Why do you think it is so important for leaders in the church not to be easily angered? "For an overseer, as God's steward, must be above reproach. He must not be arrogant or quick-tempered or a drunkard or violent or greedy for gain, but hospitable, a lover of good, self-controlled, upright, holy, and disciplined" (Titus 1:7-8).

In the book of Galatians, chapter 5, Paul spends time contrasting "walking by the Spirit" with "walking in the flesh." He says that "the works of the flesh are evident," and then he lists a number of these, including "fits of anger" as well as "enmity, strife, jealousy...rivalries, dissensions, divisions."

Then comes this stern statement: "I warn you, as I warned you before, that those who do such things will not inherit the kingdom of God" (verse 21). And then Paul provides this vivid contrast: "But the fruit of the Spirit is love, joy, peace, patience, kindness, goodness, faithfulness, gentleness, self-control" (5:22-23).

In Your Own Words

❀ How have you seen anger rooted in sinful "flesh" rather than being a function of the Holy Spirit's control in your life?

❀ What qualities that Paul lists can be especially powerful in controlling or eliminating anger?

∞

Lawrence Richards points out:

> The New Testament views unjustifiable anger and fits of rage as originating in sinful human nature. Such anger and rage, characteristic of the old nature, are to be decisively rejected by the new persons we have become in Christ...Although we may become angry, there is no question that anger is a signal to us to examine and to deal with ourselves, not justification for striking out at others.[3]

In Your Own Words

❀ What experiences helped you learn that experiencing anger is a "signal" that you need to examine yourself closely and deal at once with the problems you find within yourself?

Satan's Anger

We learn in the Scriptures that Satan is angry. Revelation 12:12 reveals one of the reasons: "Woe to you, O earth and sea, for the devil has come down to you *in great wrath*, because he knows that his time is short!" (Revelation 12:12).

Revelation 12 portrays a monstrous dragon, and identifies him as "that ancient serpent, who is called the devil and Satan, the deceiver of the whole world" (verse 9). The scene that closes the chapter describes this dragon as being "furious" as he "went off to make war...on those who keep the commandments of God and hold to the testimony of Jesus" (verse 17). Perhaps this truth about Satan's anger helps explain why Peter tells us, "Be sober-minded; be watchful. Your adversary the devil prowls around like a roaring lion, seeking someone to devour" (1 Peter 5:8).

In Your Own Words

※ Since anger appears to control Satan, how does that make you feel about being controlled by anger yourself?

※ When you get angry, how do you think that makes the devil feel?

※ Although Satan is angry, his wrath is nothing compared to the *righteous* wrath of God. In what ways do you see Satan's anger as being distinctively different from God's?

10

Anger on Display in the Scriptures

The Bible is full of men and women who struggled with anger issues. Some involved little spats, such as the occasion that caused Paul to extend a personal plea to a couple of quarreling women: "I entreat Euodia and I entreat Syntyche to agree in the Lord" (Philippians 4:2). He went on to add how "these women...have labored side by side with me in the gospel" (verse 3). And yet they were apparently having a disagreement in the church. It had not yet gotten out of hand, but the church was asked to help in this situation. They were not asked to take sides and separate the flock, but to help the two women get back into one accord.

What I find fascinating is that when we observe the stories of anger among the people in the Bible, so often they reflect the kinds of situations that cause anger to rise in us today. So let's take a closer look at some of these stories. From the facts that are presented in Scripture, think carefully about each person's anger and what lessons you can learn from the situations.

Zipporah's (and God's) Anger with Moses

After God met Moses at the burning bush and gave him instructions to go back to Egypt to lead the people of Israel out of bondage, Moses finally headed back that way with his family. But along the way, something frightening happened: "At a lodging place on the way the

Lord met him and sought to put him to death. Then Zipporah took a flint and cut off her son's foreskin and touched Moses' feet with it and said, 'Surely you are a bridegroom of blood to me!' So he let him alone. She then said, 'A bridegroom of blood,' because of the circumcision" (Exodus 4:24-26). That must have been confusing to Moses, being that God had just sent him on mission to Egypt. So why did God seek to kill him now? What's up with that?

God had gone before Moses and placed into the mind of Zipporah, Moses' wife, the reason for God's anger. She immediately carried out the mandate to circumcise their son. God's covenant with Abraham commanded this be done on the eighth day of a male child's birth, but Moses hadn't done it. So Moses' life was saved because the Lord, the great *I AM*, went before him and prepared his once-pagan wife to understand and solve the problem. And with what must have been a certain touch of anger, she remarked to Moses, "'You are a bridegroom of blood'—because of the circumcision" (verse 26 NASB).

In Your Own Words

⚅ What are your thoughts about Zipporah's anger? How can you relate this to your life?

Deborah's Anger with Barak

When I think of Deborah, I think of a fighter. Deborah was a judge and prophetess in Israel. She "arose as a mother in Israel" (Judges 5:7). She was one of the most godly of all the leaders mentioned in the book of Judges.

Deborah summoned Barak and related to him God's announcement that it was time to take care of the enemies of God's people. There was a Canaanite king, Jabin, who was tormenting them, and this king "had 900 chariots of iron and he oppressed the people of Israel cruelly for twenty years" (Judges 4:3). Deborah passed along to Barak some instructions from God. Barak was to recruit 10,000 men to go up against Sisera, the commander of the Canaanite army. God was already promising Barak the victory saying, "I will draw out Sisera, the general of Jabin's army, to meet you by the river Kishon with his chariots and his troops, and I will give him into your hand" (Judges 4:7).

Nevertheless, Barak responding by saying he was staying put unless Deborah agreed to go into battle with him. Can't you just see Deborah rolling her eyes at that? She agreed to go with Barak, but she told him he would not get credit for the victory. Instead, God was going to deliver Sisera into the hand of a woman. "Then Deborah arose and went with Barak" (4:9).

They went into combat, and as the enemy drew near, Deborah—with the heart and mind of a great military leader for God's people—turned to Barak and sounded the call to battle: "Up! For this is the day in which the LORD has given Sisera into your hand. Does not the LORD go out before you?" (Judges 4:14). I can almost hear the clarity and sharpness of her voice!

So the battle began—and God had a plan for it. He sent both an earthquake and a torrent of rain to disable the Canaanite chariots (Judges 5:4-5). The victory was God's, and it was total. But it took an angry woman to motivate the leader of the army of God's people to do his duty. And just as Deborah had prophesied, Barak did not receive credit for finishing the victory God had ordained and orchestrated that day. That honor went to a wily woman armed only with a tent peg and hammer. She killed the mighty Sisera. (You can read about it in Judges 4 and 5.)

In Your Own Words

❀ What are your thoughts about Deborah's actions? How can you relate her actions and deeds to your own?

Naomi's Anger

The lovely book of Ruth certainly doesn't start out joyfully. A man and his wife, Naomi, left the town of Bethlehem in Judah because of a famine. They went to live in the land of Moab until the famine ended.

While they were in Moab, Naomi's husband died, and so did her two sons, her only children. When Naomi returned to Bethlehem accompanied by her daughter-in-law Ruth, who refused to leave her side, Naomi's anger with God poured out in distraught words to the townspeople: "Do not call me Naomi; call me Mara [which means "bitter"], for the Almighty has dealt very bitterly with me. I went away full, and the LORD has brought me back empty. Why call me Naomi, when the LORD has testified against me and the Almighty has brought calamity upon me?" (Ruth 1:20-21).

Fortunately, we read in the rest of Ruth how God blessed the lives of Naomi and Ruth in gracious and wonderful ways. But when the good was still in the future, Naomi expressed her bitterness toward God.

In Your Own Words

✽ In what ways can you relate to the bitterness Naomi felt and expressed?

King Herod's Anger

Shortly after baby Jesus was born in Bethlehem, wise men from the east passed through Jerusalem on their way to find the prophesied Messiah.

> Herod summoned the wise men secretly and ascertained from them what time the star had appeared. And he sent them to Bethlehem, saying, "Go and search diligently for the child, and when you have found him, bring me word, that I too may come and worship him." After listening to the king, they went on their way. And behold, the star that they had seen when it rose went before them until it came to rest over the place where the child was... (Matthew 2:7-9).

After seeing the baby and worshiping him and giving him gifts, they were warned in a dream not to return to Herod. So they left for home going a different route. About that time Joseph was warned in a dream to take Mary and Jesus and flee to Egypt.

> Then Herod, when he saw that he had been tricked by the wise men, *became furious,* and he sent and killed all the male children in Bethlehem and in all that region who were two years old or under, according to the time that he had ascertained from the wise men (Matthew 2:16).

In Your Own Words

❁ What caused Herod's anger?

❁ How did that anger manifest? What words or actions did it lead to?

❁ Do you think this was appropriate anger or not? Explain.

❁ Do you know anyone who responds to anger like Herod did?

❁ Have you ever experienced and/or responded to anger like Herods?

An Angry King in Parable

Jesus told a parable that involves anger:

> The kingdom of heaven may be compared to a king who wished to settle accounts with his servants. When he began to settle, one was brought to him who owed him ten thousand talents. And since he could not pay, his master ordered him to be sold, with his wife and children and all that he had, and payment to be made.
>
> So the servant fell on his knees, imploring him, "Have patience with me, and I will pay you everything."
>
> And out of pity for him, the master of that servant released him and forgave him the debt.
>
> But when that same servant went out, he found one of his fellow servants who owed him a hundred denarii, and

seizing him, he began to choke him, saying, "Pay what you owe."

So his fellow servant fell down and pleaded with him, "Have patience with me, and I will pay you."

He refused and went and put him in prison until he should pay the debt.

When his fellow servants saw what had taken place, they were greatly distressed, and they went and reported to their master all that had taken place.

Then his master summoned him and said to him, "You wicked servant! I forgave you all that debt because you pleaded with me. And should not you have had mercy on your fellow servant, as I had mercy on you?" And *in anger* his master delivered him to the jailers, until he should pay all his debt (Matthew 18:23-34).

In Your Own Words

❀ What caused the master's anger at the end of the story?

❀ How did that anger manifest? What words or actions did it lead to?

❀ Do you think this was appropriate anger or not? Explain.

❀ Is this like anyone's anger you know?

❀ Is this like any anger you've experienced?

Another Angry King

Here's another story Jesus told involving anger:

The kingdom of heaven may be compared to a king who gave a wedding feast for his son, and sent his servants to call those who were invited to the wedding feast, but they would not come. Again he sent other servants, saying,

"Tell those who are invited, See, I have prepared my dinner, my oxen and my fat calves have been slaughtered, and
everything is ready. Come to the wedding feast." But they
paid no attention and went off, one to his farm, another
to his business, while the rest seized his servants, treated
them shamefully, and killed them.

The king was angry, and he sent his troops and
destroyed those murderers and burned their city. Then he
said to his servants, "The wedding feast is ready, but those
invited were not worthy. Go therefore to the main roads
and invite to the wedding feast as many as you find."

And those servants went out into the roads and gathered all whom they found, both bad and good. So the
wedding hall was filled with guests (Matthew 22:2-10).

In Your Own Words

❊ What caused this king's anger?

❊ How did that anger manifest? What words or actions did it lead to?

❊ Do you think this was appropriate anger or not? Explain.

❊ Is it like anyone's anger you know of?

❊ Is it like any anger you've experienced?

An Angry Brother

In the following famous story from Jesus, notice the angry reaction of the older brother.

There was a man who had two sons. And the younger of
them said to his father, "Father, give me the share of property that is coming to me."

And he divided his property between them.

Not many days later, the younger son gathered all he had and took a journey into a far country, and there he squandered his property in reckless living. And when he had spent everything, a severe famine arose in that country, and he began to be in need. So he went and hired himself out to one of the citizens of that country, who sent him into his fields to feed pigs. And he was longing to be fed with the pods that the pigs ate, and no one gave him anything. But when he came to himself, he said, "How many of my father's hired servants have more than enough bread, but I perish here with hunger! I will arise and go to my father, and I will say to him, 'Father, I have sinned against heaven and before you. I am no longer worthy to be called your son. Treat me as one of your hired servants.'" And he arose and came to his father.

But while he was still a long way off, his father saw him and felt compassion, and ran and embraced him and kissed him. And the son said to him, "Father, I have sinned against heaven and before you. I am no longer worthy to be called your son."

But the father said to his servants, "Bring quickly the best robe, and put it on him, and put a ring on his hand, and shoes on his feet. And bring the fattened calf and kill it, and let us eat and celebrate. For this my son was dead, and is alive again; he was lost, and is found." And they began to celebrate.

Now his older son was in the field, and as he came and drew near to the house, he heard music and dancing. And he called one of the servants and asked what these things meant.

And he said to him, "Your brother has come, and your father has killed the fattened calf, because he has received him back safe and sound."

But *he was angry* and refused to go in. His father came out and entreated him, but he answered his father, "Look, these many years I have served you, and I never disobeyed your command, yet you never gave me a young goat, that

I might celebrate with my friends. But when this son of yours came, who has devoured your property with prostitutes, you killed the fattened calf for him!"

And he said to him, "Son, you are always with me, and all that is mine is yours. It was fitting to celebrate and be glad, for this your brother was dead, and is alive; he was lost, and is found" (Luke 15:11-32).

In Your Own Words

❄ What was the real cause of the older brother's anger?

❄ How did that anger manifest? What words or actions did it lead to?

❄ Do you think this was appropriate anger or not? Explain.

❄ Is it like anyone's anger you know of?

❄ Is it like any anger you've experienced?

Jesus Provokes Anger

Jesus had a way of making some people angry—such as on this occasion in His hometown:

> And [Jesus] came to Nazareth, where he had been brought up. And as was his custom, he went to the synagogue on the Sabbath day, and he stood up to read. And the scroll of the prophet Isaiah was given to him. He unrolled the scroll and found the place where it was written,
>
> > "The Spirit of the Lord is upon me, because he has anointed me to proclaim good news to the poor. He has sent me to proclaim liberty to the captives and recovering of sight to the blind, to set at liberty those who are oppressed, to proclaim the year of the Lord's favor."

And he rolled up the scroll and gave it back to the attendant and sat down. And the eyes of all in the synagogue were fixed on him. And he began to say to them, "Today this Scripture has been fulfilled in your hearing."

And all spoke well of him and marveled at the gracious words that were coming from his mouth. And they said, "Is not this Joseph's son?"

And he said to them, "Doubtless you will quote to me this proverb, 'Physician, heal yourself.' What we have heard you did at Capernaum, do here in your hometown as well." And he said, "Truly, I say to you, no prophet is acceptable in his hometown. But in truth, I tell you, there were many widows in Israel in the days of Elijah, when the heavens were shut up three years and six months, and a great famine came over all the land, and Elijah was sent to none of them but only to Zarephath, in the land of Sidon, to a woman who was a widow. And there were many lepers in Israel in the time of the prophet Elisha, and none of them was cleansed, but only Naaman the Syrian."

When they heard these things, all in the synagogue were *filled with wrath*. And they rose up and drove him out of the town and brought him to the brow of the hill on which their town was built, so that they could throw him down the cliff. But passing through their midst, he went away (Luke 4:16-30).

In Your Own Words

❋ What caused the anger of the people in the Nazareth synagogue?

❋ How did that anger manifest? What words or actions did it lead to?

❋ What was wrong about their anger?

❋ Is their anger like anyone's anger you know of?

❋ Is it like any anger you've experienced?

An Angry Moses

Now, let's go back to the Old Testament and observe some angry people there. First, let's look again at Moses. The time is when God sent manna from heaven to feed the hungry Israelites in the desert.

> In the morning dew lay around the camp. And when the dew had gone up, there was on the face of the wilderness a fine, flake-like thing, fine as frost on the ground...
>
> And Moses said to them, "It is the bread that the LORD has given you to eat. This is what the LORD has commanded: 'Gather of it, each one of you, as much as he can eat. You shall each take an omer, according to the number of the persons that each of you has in his tent.'"
>
> And the people of Israel did so. They gathered some more, some less. But when they measured it with an omer, whoever gathered much had nothing left over, and whoever gathered little had no lack. Each of them gathered as much as he could eat.
>
> And Moses said to them, "Let no one leave any of it over till the morning."
>
> But they did not listen to Moses. Some left part of it till the morning, and it bred worms and stank. And *Moses was angry with them.*
>
> Morning by morning they gathered it, each as much as he could eat; but when the sun grew hot, it melted (Exodus 16:13-21).

In Your Own Words

❀ What caused Moses to be angry?

❀ Do you think this was appropriate anger or not? Explain.

❀ Is it like anyone's anger you know of?

❀ Is it like any anger you've experienced?

Samuel's Anger

Hundreds of years after Moses, the prophet Samuel experienced anger when Saul—the man God told Samuel to anoint as Israel's first king—disobeyed God. You can read the full story in 1 Samuel 15. Here are some key portions:

> The word of the LORD came to Samuel: "I regret that I have made Saul king, for he has turned back from following me and has not performed my commandments." And *Samuel was angry,* and he cried to the LORD all night (1 Samuel 15:10-11).

> Samuel said to Saul, "Stop! I will tell you what the LORD said to me this night" (verse 16).

> And Samuel said, "Has the LORD as great delight in burnt offerings and sacrifices, as in obeying the voice of the LORD? Behold, to obey is better than sacrifice, and to listen than the fat of rams...Because you have rejected the word of the LORD, he has also rejected you from being king" (verses 22-23).

> As Samuel turned to go away, Saul seized the skirt of his robe, and it tore. And Samuel said to him, "The LORD has torn the kingdom of Israel from you this day and has given it to a neighbor of yours, who is better than you..." (verses 27-28).

> Then Samuel went to Ramah, and Saul went up to his house in Gibeah of Saul. And Samuel did not see Saul again until the day of his death, but Samuel grieved over Saul (verses 34-35).

In Your Own Words

❦ What caused Samuel's anger?

❦ How did that anger manifest? What words or actions did it lead to?

❧ Do you think this was appropriate anger or not? Explain.

❧ Is it like anyone's anger you know of?

❧ Is it like any anger you've experienced?

❧ What guidelines do you see in Samuel's example about the proper way to process anger?

David's Anger Toward God

Samuel anointed David to become king instead of Saul. And King David was someone who also experienced anger. Here is one of the most interesting and complex disclosures of his anger. It occurs when David and his men brought back the ark of God to Jerusalem (it had been captured by the Philistines):

> David again gathered all the chosen men of Israel, thirty thousand. And David arose and went with all the people who were with him from Baale-judah to bring up from there the ark of God, which is called by the name of the LORD of hosts who sits enthroned on the cherubim. And they carried the ark of God on a new cart and brought it out of the house of Abinadab, which was on the hill. And Uzzah and Ahio, the sons of Abinadab, were driving the new cart, with the ark of God, and Ahio went before the ark.
>
> And David and all the house of Israel were making merry before the LORD, with songs and lyres and harps and tambourines and castanets and cymbals. And when they came to the threshing floor of Nacon, Uzzah put out his hand to the ark of God and took hold of it, for the oxen stumbled. And *the anger of the* LORD was kindled against Uzzah, and God struck him down there because of his error, and he died there beside the ark of God.
>
> And *David was angry* because the LORD had burst forth against Uzzah. And that place is called Perez-uzzah, to this day. And David was afraid of the LORD that day,

and he said, "How can the ark of the LORD come to me?"
So David was not willing to take the ark of the LORD into
the city of David. But David took it aside to the house of
Obed-edom the Gittite (2 Samuel 6:1-10).

In Your Own Words

❃ What caused David's anger?

❃ How did that anger manifest? What words or actions did it lead to?

❃ Do you think David's anger was appropriate or not? Explain.

❃ Is it like anyone's anger you know of?

❃ Is it like any anger you've experienced?

An Army Officer's Anger

In the days of the prophet Elisha, the commander of Syria's army,
a man named Naaman, contracted leprosy. Naaman had heard about
Elisha, and he asked the king of Syria for permission to travel to Israel
to seek a miraculous cure. The king of Syria agreed and sent along a
letter directed to Israel's king. Here's what happened next:

> So [Naaman] went, taking with him ten talents of silver,
> six thousand shekels of gold, and ten changes of clothing.
> And he brought the letter to the king of Israel, which read,
> "When this letter reaches you, know that I have sent to you
> Naaman my servant, that you may cure him of his leprosy."
>
> And when the king of Israel read the letter, he tore his
> clothes and said, "Am I God, to kill and to make alive,
> that this man sends word to me to cure a man of his lep-
> rosy? Only consider, and see how he is seeking a quarrel
> with me."
>
> But when Elisha the man of God heard that the king
> of Israel had torn his clothes, he sent to the king, saying,

"Why have you torn your clothes? Let him come now to me, that he may know that there is a prophet in Israel."

So Naaman came with his horses and chariots and stood at the door of Elisha's house. And Elisha sent a messenger to him, saying, "Go and wash in the Jordan seven times, and your flesh shall be restored, and you shall be clean."

But *Naaman was angry* and went away, saying, "Behold, I thought that he would surely come out to me and stand and call upon the name of the LORD his God, and wave his hand over the place and cure the leper. Are not Abana and Pharpar, the rivers of Damascus, better than all the waters of Israel? Could I not wash in them and be clean?" So he turned and *went away in a rage.*

But his servants came near and said to him, "My father, it is a great word the prophet has spoken to you; will you not do it? Has he actually said to you, 'Wash, and be clean'?"

So he went down and dipped himself seven times in the Jordan, according to the word of the man of God, and his flesh was restored like the flesh of a little child, and he was clean (2 Kings 5:5-14).

In Your Own Words

❅ What caused Naaman's anger?

❅ What did his anger reveal about him?

❅ How did his anger manifest? What words or actions did it lead to?

❅ Do you think this was appropriate anger or not? Explain.

❅ Is it like anyone's anger you know of?

❅ Is it like any anger you've experienced?

❅ What did it take to overcome his anger?

More Royal Anger

One of King David's descendants was King Asa, who "did what was good and right in the eyes of the LORD his God" (2 Chronicles 14:2). The Bible commends him for his faithfulness and his effective leadership. Asa built up a large army, all of them mighty men of valor. On one occasion, "Zerah the Ethiopian came out against them with an army of a million men and 300 chariots, and came as far as Mareshah. And Asa went out to meet him, and they drew up their lines of battle in the Valley of Zephathah at Mareshah" (verses 9-10).

Next we see the God-centered way Asa approaches this battle:

> Asa cried to the LORD his God, "O LORD, there is none like you to help, between the mighty and the weak. Help us, O LORD our God, for we rely on you, and in your name we have come against this multitude. O LORD, you are our God; let not man prevail against you."
>
> So the LORD defeated the Ethiopians before Asa and before Judah, and the Ethiopians fled (verses 11-12).

But when Asa became older, his devotion to the Lord took a serious downturn. When Judah faced further military threats, Asa decided to form a costly alliance with the king of Syria (instead of entirely trusting God). And Asa was called onto the carpet for it:

> At that time Hanani the seer came to Asa king of Judah and said to him, "Because you relied on the king of Syria, and did not rely on the LORD your God, the army of the king of Syria has escaped you. Were not the Ethiopians and the Libyans a huge army with very many chariots and horsemen? Yet because you relied on the LORD, he gave them into your hand. For the eyes of the LORD run to and fro throughout the whole earth, to give strong support to those whose heart is blameless toward him. You have done foolishly in this, for from now on you will have wars."
>
> Then *Asa was angry* with the seer and put him in the stocks in prison, for he was *in a rage* with him because of

this. And Asa inflicted cruelties upon some of the people
at the same time (2 Chronicles 16:7-10).

In Your Own Words

❀ What caused King Asa's anger and rage?

❀ How did that anger manifest? What words or actions did it lead to?

❀ Do you think this was appropriate anger or not? Explain.

❀ Is it like anyone's anger you know of?

❀ Is it like any anger you've experienced?

❀

Often it seems that some of the angriest people are those who are
most aware—down deep in their souls—of how terribly wrong their
actions have been.

❀ Do you agree? Explain.

❀ How could Asa's story be an illustration of this?

King Uzziah's Anger

Another of David's descendants was King Uzziah, a very capable king. We see many of his accomplishments listed in 2 Chronicles
26, which adds that his fame spread far and his power grew. But then
came a moment of anger that changed his life forever:

> But when [King Uzziah] was strong, he grew proud, to his
> destruction. For he was unfaithful to the LORD his God
> and entered the temple of the LORD to burn incense on
> the altar of incense.

But Azariah the priest went in after him, with eighty priests of the LORD who were men of valor, and they withstood King Uzziah and said to him, "It is not for you, Uzziah, to burn incense to the LORD, but for the priests the sons of Aaron, who are consecrated to burn incense. Go out of the sanctuary, for you have done wrong, and it will bring you no honor from the LORD God."

Then *Uzziah was angry*. Now he had a censer in his hand to burn incense, and when he became *angry* with the priests, leprosy broke out on his forehead in the presence of the priests in the house of the LORD, by the altar of incense.

And Azariah the chief priest and all the priests looked at him, and behold, he was leprous in his forehead! And they rushed him out quickly, and he himself hurried to go out, because the LORD had struck him.

And King Uzziah was a leper to the day of his death, and being a leper lived in a separate house, for he was excluded from the house of the LORD (2 Chronicles 26:16-21).

In Your Own Words

❊ What caused Uzziah's anger?

❊ How did that anger manifest? What words or actions did it lead to?

❊ Do you think this was appropriate anger or not? Explain.

❊ Is it like anyone's anger you know of?

❊ Is it like any anger you've experienced?

❊ Sometimes it seems that pride is one of the most potent ingredients behind people's anger. Do you agree? Explain.

❊ If you agreed, how could Uzziah's story be an illustration of this?

Nehemiah's Anger

Centuries later, when God's people had returned from their exile in Babylon and were rebuilding and restoring Jerusalem, we see more instances of anger during the time of Nehemiah. You'll recall that Nehemiah was the godly man the Lord called to lead the people of Jerusalem in rebuilding its walls and gates. Once that work got underway, there was major opposition—*angry* opposition—from some of the heathen leaders who lived nearby:

> Now when Sanballat heard that we were building the wall, *he was angry and greatly enraged*, and he jeered at the Jews. And he said in the presence of his brothers and of the army of Samaria, "What are these feeble Jews doing? Will they restore it for themselves? Will they sacrifice? Will they finish up in a day? Will they revive the stones out of the heaps of rubbish, and burned ones at that?"
>
> Tobiah the Ammonite was beside him, and he said, "Yes, what they are building—if a fox goes up on it he will break down their stone wall!"
>
> [But Nehemiah prayed:] Hear, O our God, for we are despised. Turn back their taunt on their own heads and give them up to be plundered in a land where they are captives. Do not cover their guilt, and let not their sin be blotted out from your sight, for they have provoked you to anger in the presence of the builders.
>
> So we built the wall. And all the wall was joined together to half its height, for the people had a mind to work.
>
> But when Sanballat and Tobiah and the Arabs and the Ammonites and the Ashdodites heard that the repairing of the walls of Jerusalem was going forward and that the breaches were beginning to be closed, *they were very angry*. And they all plotted together to come and fight against Jerusalem and to cause confusion in it.
>
> And we prayed to our God and set a guard as a protection against them day and night (Nehemiah 4:1-9).

In Your Own Words

❀ What caused the anger of Sanballat and his cohorts?

❀ How did that anger manifest? What words or actions did it lead to?

❀ Do you think their anger was appropriate or not? Explain.

❀ Is it like anyone's anger you know of?

❀ Is it like any anger you've experienced?

❀ Why do you think doing the Lord's work often causes angry opposition from unbelievers?

Anger in Babylon

Babylon's King Nebuchadnezzar displayed his hot temper more than once. He conquered Jerusalem and had some of the best of the Israelite people exiled to Babylon, including a teen named Daniel.

On one occasion the king was having disturbing dreams. "His spirit was troubled, and his sleep left him" (Daniel 2:1). He decided to ask for help. That's a reasonable thing to do, right?

> Then the king commanded that the magicians, the enchanters, the sorcerers, and the Chaldeans be summoned to tell the king his dreams. So they came in and stood before the king. And the king said to them, "I had a dream, and my spirit is troubled to know the dream."
>
> Then the Chaldeans said to the king in Aramaic, "O king, live forever! Tell your servants the dream, and we will show the interpretation."
>
> The king answered and said to the Chaldeans, "The word from me is firm: if you do not make known to me the dream and its interpretation, you shall be torn limb from limb, and your houses shall be laid in ruins. But if you show the dream and its interpretation, you shall

receive from me gifts and rewards and great honor. Therefore show me the dream and its interpretation."

They answered a second time and said, "Let the king tell his servants the dream, and we will show its interpretation."

The king answered and said, "I know with certainty that you are trying to gain time, because you see that the word from me is firm—if you do not make the dream known to me, there is but one sentence for you. You have agreed to speak lying and corrupt words before me till the times change. Therefore tell me the dream, and I shall know that you can show me its interpretation."

The Chaldeans answered the king and said, "There is not a man on earth who can meet the king's demand, for no great and powerful king has asked such a thing of any magician or enchanter or Chaldean. The thing that the king asks is difficult, and no one can show it to the king except the gods, whose dwelling is not with flesh."

Because of this *the king was angry and very furious*, and commanded that all the wise men of Babylon be destroyed. So the decree went out, and the wise men were about to be killed; and they sought Daniel and his companions, to kill them (Daniel 2:1-13).

In Your Own Words

❀ What caused Nebuchadnezzar's anger?

❀ How did that anger manifest? What words or actions did it lead to?

❀ Do you think this was appropriate anger or not? Explain.

❀ Is it like anyone's anger you know of?

❀ Is it like any anger you've experienced?

Anger Rages in Babylon

King Nebuchadnezzar's story continues. Daniel saves the lives of the wise men by intervening. He goes before Nebuchadnezzar and announces, "There is a God in heaven who reveals mysteries" (Daniel 2:28). And then the young Israelite tells the king the exact details of his dreams as well as their meaning. So Nebuchadnezzar's anger leaves him—but not for long.

Nebuchadnezzar orders that a huge statue of gold be set up and commands that everybody must bow down and worship it.

> At that time certain Chaldeans came forward and maliciously accused the Jews. They declared to King Nebuchadnezzar, "O king, live forever! You, O king, have made a decree, that every man who hears the sound of the horn, pipe, lyre, trigon, harp, bagpipe, and every kind of music, shall fall down and worship the golden image. And whoever does not fall down and worship shall be cast into a burning fiery furnace. There are certain Jews whom you have appointed over the affairs of the province of Babylon: Shadrach, Meshach, and Abednego. These men, O king, pay no attention to you; they do not serve your gods or worship the golden image that you have set up."
>
> Then *Nebuchadnezzar in furious rage* commanded that Shadrach, Meshach, and Abednego be brought. So they brought these men before the king.
>
> Nebuchadnezzar answered and said to them, "Is it true, O Shadrach, Meshach, and Abednego, that you do not serve my gods or worship the golden image that I have set up? Now if you are ready when you hear the sound of the horn, pipe, lyre, trigon, harp, bagpipe, and every kind of music, to fall down and worship the image that I have made, well and good. But if you do not worship, you shall immediately be cast into a burning fiery furnace. And who is the god who will deliver you out of my hands?"
>
> Shadrach, Meshach, and Abednego answered and said to the king, "O Nebuchadnezzar, we have no need to

answer you in this matter. If this be so, our God whom we serve is able to deliver us from the burning fiery furnace, and he will deliver us out of your hand, O king. But if not, be it known to you, O king, that we will not serve your gods or worship the golden image that you have set up."

Then Nebuchadnezzar was *filled with fury,* and the expression of his face was changed against Shadrach, Meshach, and Abednego. He ordered the furnace heated seven times more than it was usually heated. And he ordered some of the mighty men of his army to bind Shadrach, Meshach, and Abednego, and to cast them into the burning fiery furnace. Then these men were bound in their cloaks, their tunics, their hats, and their other garments, and they were thrown into the burning fiery furnace.

Because the king's order was urgent and the furnace overheated, the flame of the fire killed those men who took up Shadrach, Meshach, and Abednego. And these three men, Shadrach, Meshach, and Abednego, fell bound into the burning fiery furnace (Daniel 3:8-23).

In Your Own Words

�֎ Nebuchadnezzar's anger was almost as hot as that furnace! What caused it?

✖ How did that anger manifest? What words or actions did it lead to?

✖ Do you think this was appropriate anger or not? Explain.

✖ Is it like anyone's anger you know of?

✖ Is it like any anger you've experienced?

∽

Once again, Nebuchadnezzar's anger was defused by a miracle

from God—this time when Shadrach, Meshach, and Abednego were preserved unharmed in the midst of that blazing furnace!

So you see there really is a lot of anger in the Bible!

In Your Own Words

⊠ From all these incidents of anger we've looked at, what are the most significant themes and lessons you've observed?

⊂⊃

Lord, please help me not fall prey to anger that doesn't honor You. When unrighteous anger rises up inside me, let me know its causes. Remind me to turn to You and ask for Your forgiveness. Do not let me be counted among the people mentioned in Your Word who became angry and sinned. Please save me from myself. In Jesus' name. Amen.

11

Observing God's Anger

In this chapter we're going to spend some time taking a closer look at the anger of God. Now you may be thinking, *What does God's anger have to do with my anger?* But as we look into God's Word, we'll find so much there about God's anger that will help us gain a much wider and deeper perspective for understanding our own anger by comparison.

Yes, it's *good* for you and me to give some careful thought to the anger of the Lord. It may not sound like a pleasant or inviting subject, but I suspect we'll end up being surprised by the positive truths we'll be directed toward as we survey God's wrath.

In Psalm 90, which is entitled "a prayer of Moses, the man of God," Moses asks the Lord this provocative question: "Who considers the power of *your anger,* and *your wrath* according to the fear of you?" (verse 11). The implied answer is that nobody really considers and recognizes the force of God's anger as clearly as he or she should.

God's anger is serious business. This fact comes through clearly again and again in Scripture. Listen to these words from the prophet Nahum: "Who can stand before *his indignation*? Who can endure the heat of *his anger*? *His wrath* is poured out like fire, and the rocks are broken into pieces by him" (Nahum 1:6). And from the prophet Jeremiah: "The LORD is the true God; he is the living God and the everlasting King. At *his wrath* the earth quakes, and the nations cannot endure *his indignation*" (Jeremiah 10:10). And from the psalmist

Asaph: "But you, you are to be feared! Who can stand before you when once *your anger* is roused?" (Psalm 76:7).

David recognized the seriousness of God's anger when he sang and prayed, "O LORD, rebuke me not in *your anger,* nor discipline me in *your wrath*" (Psalm 6:1; 38:1). David also tells us, "God is a righteous judge, and a God who feels *indignation* every day" (Psalm 7:11).

In Your Own Words

❧ From these passages that emphasize the seriousness of God's anger, what do you think is most significant for you to understand?

☙

Meanwhile, one thing we learn in the New Testament is that God's anger is an important element in our proper understanding of governmental authority. Have you ever thought about that? Look over this passage:

> Let every person be subject to the governing authorities. For there is no authority except from God, and those that exist have been instituted by God. Therefore whoever resists the authorities resists what God has appointed, and those who resist will incur judgment. For rulers are not a terror to good conduct, but to bad. Would you have no fear of the one who is in authority? Then do what is good, and you will receive his approval, for he is God's servant for your good. But if you do wrong, be afraid, for he does not bear the sword in vain. For he is the servant of God, an avenger who carries out *God's wrath* on the wrongdoer. Therefore one must be in subjection, not only to avoid God's wrath but also for the sake of conscience (Romans 13:1-5).

We see that when a governing authority punishes someone, the government is carrying out God's wrath.

In Your Own Words

▓ What could this be teaching you about how God's wrath is operating in the world today?

▓ Why do you think it is important to understand governing authority in this way?

Reasons for God's Anger

"God's anger is no capricious thing, nor is it expressed in temper tantrums. God's anger is provoked: it is his righteous response to specific human failures and sin…God's anger is a measured response to sin."[1]

Why does God get angry? Let's look at a sobering passage, where the Lord on Mount Sinai is giving instructions through Moses:

> You shall not wrong a sojourner or oppress him, for you were sojourners in the land of Egypt. You shall not mistreat any widow or fatherless child. If you do mistreat them, and they cry out to me, I will surely hear their cry, and *my wrath will burn,* and I will kill you with the sword, and your wives shall become widows and your children fatherless (Exodus 22:21-24).

In Your Own Words

▓ According to these verses in Exodus, what is one thing that causes God to be angry?

▓ What does this say to you about God's character?

∞

God's people are clearly warned through Moses not to provoke His wrath through the sin of idolatry:

Take care, lest you forget the covenant of the LORD your God, which he made with you, and make a carved image, the form of anything that the LORD your God has forbidden you. For the LORD your God is a consuming fire, a jealous God...If you act corruptly by making a carved image in the form of anything, and by doing what is evil in the sight of the LORD your God, so as to *provoke him to anger,* I call heaven and earth to witness against you today, that the LORD will scatter you among the peoples (Deuteronomy 4:23-27).

After the people of Israel had settled the Promised Land, this warning against idolatry was repeated by their new leader, Joshua:

Just as all the good things that the LORD your God promised concerning you have been fulfilled for you, so the LORD will bring upon you all the evil things, until he has destroyed you from off this good land that the LORD your God has given you, if you transgress the covenant of the LORD your God, which he commanded you, and go and serve other gods and bow down to them. Then *the anger of the LORD* will be kindled against you, and you shall perish quickly from off the good land that he has given to you (Joshua 23:15-16).

In Your Own Words

❀ What do these warnings teach you about God's anger?

❀ What does it say about His character?

∞

When God spoke to Moses out of a burning bush and called him to go and lead His people out of Egypt, Moses took it upon himself to decline the offer. He said, "Oh, my Lord, please send someone else" (Exodus 4:13). This did *not* trigger from God the response Moses was looking for. Instead we read: "Then the *anger of the LORD was kindled* against Moses" (verse 14).

In Your Own Words

❧ What does this response demonstrate about God's expectations of those He calls to leadership?

∽

In Scripture we also observe that once God's anger is made apparent to His people—through the punishment and affliction He sends to discipline them—the people pay more attention to Him. Look at these words spoken through the prophet Ezekiel about the coming destruction of Jerusalem:

> Thus shall *my anger* spend itself, and I will vent *my fury* upon them and satisfy myself. And they shall know that I am the LORD—that I have spoken in my jealousy—when I spend *my fury* upon them (Ezekiel 5:13).

"They shall know that *I am the LORD*"! God wanted His people to give Him the glory and worship and recognition He deserved, even if it would take severe measures to bring this about.

In Your Own Words

❧ What further thoughts about God's anger does this verse from Ezekiel bring to your mind?

Slow to Anger

In your acquaintance with the Old Testament, I'm sure you recall the occasion when the children of Israel made a golden calf to worship—at the very same time when their leader, Moses, was on the mountaintop talking with God on their behalf.

Now the Lord knew what was going on before Moses did. And there on the mountaintop, He revealed His anger to Moses:

> And the LORD said to Moses, "Go down, for your people, whom you brought up out of the land of Egypt, have corrupted themselves. They have turned aside quickly out of the way that I commanded them. They have made for themselves a golden calf and have worshiped it and sacrificed to it and said, 'These are your gods, O Israel, who brought you up out of the land of Egypt!'" And the LORD said to Moses, "I have seen this people, and behold, it is a stiff-necked people. Now therefore let me alone, that *my wrath may burn hot* against them and I may consume them, in order that I may make a great nation of you" (Exodus 32:7-10).

In Your Own Words

❦ As you read that passage and reflect on it, why do you think the people's actions were so conducive to this kind of anger on God's part?

❦ What does this highlight about God's character?

❦ What do you learn about righteous anger in this instance?

❦ Why do you think God told this to Moses? What did He want Moses to learn?

∞

Now let's see how Moses responded:

> But Moses implored the LORD his God and said, "O LORD, *why does your wrath burn hot against your people*, whom you have brought out of the land of Egypt with great power and with a mighty hand? Why should the Egyptians say, 'With evil intent did he bring them out, to kill them in the mountains and to consume them from

the face of the earth'? *Turn from your burning anger* and relent from this disaster against your people. Remember Abraham, Isaac, and Israel, your servants, to whom you swore by your own self, and said to them, 'I will multiply your offspring as the stars of heaven, and all this land that I have promised I will give to your offspring, and they shall inherit it forever'" (Exodus 32:11-13).

In Your Own Words

🢒 What do you think is the best answer to the first question Moses asks the Lord in those verses?

🢒 What would you say is the most important thing Moses understands about God's anger?

∞

God listened to Moses' prayer, and He did exactly what Moses asked Him to do: "And the LORD relented from the disaster that he had spoken of bringing on his people" (Exodus 32:14).

In Your Own Words

🢒 What does this tell you about God's character and about His anger?

∞

Then Moses decided it was time to head back down the mountain. He picked up the stone tablets with the Ten Commandments engraved on them by God's finger. His assistant, Joshua, was with him. Let's see what happens next:

> Moses turned and went down from the mountain with the two tablets of the testimony...When Joshua heard the noise of the people as they shouted, he said to Moses, "There is a

noise of war in the camp." But he said, "It is not the sound of shouting for victory, or the sound of the cry of defeat, but the sound of singing that I hear." And as soon as he came near the camp and saw the calf and the dancing, *Moses' anger burned hot,* and he threw the tablets out of his hands and broke them at the foot of the mountain. He took the calf that they had made and burned it (Exodus 32:15-20).

In Your Own Words

❧ How would you explain and evaluate this display of anger on the part of Moses? Was it righteous? Justifiable? Why or why not?

❧ From what you've seen in the Scriptures so far, how would you compare and contrast God's anger with the kinds of anger you've experienced in your life?

∞

Later we find Moses and the people of God in another instructive situation for us, one that has some similarities to the incident involving the golden calf. In Numbers 13 we read how Moses sent 12 scouts into the land of Canaan to see what the people of God would be getting into once they got there. Remember the story? When the spies returned with their reports, they told everybody what a grand and fruitful land Canaan was—flowing with milk and honey. However, several of the spies had gotten spooked by the military defenses they had observed. And the more they thought about this and the more they talked about it, the more scared they became. And that got the people of Israel worried as well. Pretty soon the situation was out of control. The people were in flat-out rebellion against the leadership of Moses of Aaron—and against the Lord as well.

Moses and Aaron tried to reason with everybody. So did Joshua and Caleb (the only two spies who weren't scared). But that didn't work. The people were ready to stone Moses and Aaron and bury them under a pile of rocks. For so long these people had been unruly and complaining about this and that. For example, just a few chapters earlier, we read: "And the people complained in the hearing of the LORD about their misfortunes, and when the LORD heard it, *his anger was kindled,* and the fire of the Lord burned among them and consumed some outlying parts of the camp" (Numbers 11:1).

In Your Own Words

❀ Why do you think complaining on the part of God's people is something that earns God's anger?

∾

And now with the people's new eruption over the report from the spies, well, it just seemed like the last straw. So God spoke to Moses like He had done on Mount Sinai: "And the LORD said to Moses, 'How long will this people despise me? And how long will they not believe in me, in spite of all the signs that I have done among them? I will strike them with the pestilence and disinherit them'" (Numbers 14:11-12).

The Lord decided He would get rid of His people and proceed to Plan B. He was going to start all over again. He would build up a new nation from Moses (verse 12), just as He had done over the past several centuries using Abraham and his descendants.

But Moses once again begged God to spare His people. And as he prayed and pleaded, he brought up something very important in regard to God's anger:

> And now, please let the power of the Lord be great as you have promised, saying, "*The LORD is slow to anger* and abounding in steadfast love, forgiving iniquity and transgression..." Please pardon the iniquity of this people, according to the greatness of your steadfast love, just as you have forgiven this people, from Egypt until now (Numbers 14:17-19).

God's anger is a *slow* anger! Moses *knew* this was true. He had seen the truth of it again and again in the gracious and compassionate and merciful way God responded to His people in their weaknesses and their sinfulness. But Moses also knew this was true because God told him so.

This happened earlier, right after the incident with the golden calf. Moses had continued praying for the people and praying for the Lord's guidance for them. He had also asked if he could somehow experience God's presence in an especially close way. Moses said to the Lord, "Show me now your ways" and "Show me your glory" (Exodus 33:13,18). God answered by saying that His face was so holy and glorious that the sight of it would be fatal for a mortal like Moses. However, God agreed to give Moses a limited glimpse.

God told Moses to bring two more stone tablets up the mountain with him (to replace the set Moses had smashed), and He would engrave the Ten Commandments on these new tablets. After Moses carried those fresh stone blanks up the mountainside, the Lord came down to that mountain in a cloud, and Moses heard His voice: "The LORD, the LORD, a God merciful and gracious, *slow to anger,* and abounding in steadfast love and faithfulness, keeping steadfast love for thousands, forgiving iniquity and transgression and sin" (Exodus 34:6-7).

In Your Own Words

🕸 From these words spoken by the Lord to Moses, what should you keep in mind when you think about God's anger?

🕸 Why do you think this is this important?

🕸 What does that phrase "slow to anger" mean to you?

⌒

"This significant statement [Exodus 34:6-7] places anger in a distinctive relationship with other qualities of the Lord. He is compassionate, gracious, loving, faithful, forgiving, just. God's anger never dominates to the extent that these other character traits no longer function."[2]

This fact that God is *slow* to anger is strongly emphasized in the Old Testament. David sang it about it in three of his psalms that have been preserved for us:

> But you, O LORD, are a God merciful and gracious, *slow to anger* and abounding in steadfast love and faithfulness (Psalm 86:15).

> The LORD is merciful and gracious, *slow to anger* and abounding in steadfast love (103:8).

> The LORD is gracious and merciful, *slow to anger* and abounding in steadfast love (145:8).

Centuries later, the prophet Jonah recalled this truth after he saw the people of mean and mighty Nineveh repent, thereby escaping God's impending and awful judgment: "And he prayed to the LORD and said, 'O LORD...I knew that you are a gracious God and merciful, *slow to anger* and abounding in steadfast love, and relenting from disaster'" (Jonah 4:2).

And when the later generations of Nineveh returned to their evil ways, the slowness of God's anger was a key part of the message given to them through the prophet Nahum: "The LORD is *slow to anger* and great in power, and the LORD will by no means clear the guilty. His way is in whirlwind and storm, and the clouds are the dust of his feet" (Nahum 1:3).

Likewise God's slowness to anger is what the prophet Joel reminded God's people about as he pleaded for them to repent of their waywardness: "Return to the LORD, your God, for he is gracious and merciful, *slow to anger,* and abounding in steadfast love; and he relents over disaster" (Joel 2:13).

And much later, after God's people had been exiled to Babylon for their sins and idolatry, and then finally brought back to the Promised Land, God's slowness to anger is what the godly leader Nehemiah remembered as he prayed on their behalf and confessed their continued sins: "But you are a God ready to forgive, gracious and merciful, *slow to anger* and abounding in steadfast love" (Nehemiah 9:17).

Think deeply about this truth that we find repeated so often in the Old Testament. We know that whatever provokes the anger of our holy and loving God, His anger must always be justifiable and righteous and appropriate. He certainly has every right to be angry over the corrupt and rebellious thoughts and actions of the human beings He created and surrounded with so much grace and love and good things. And yet the Lord is *slow* about His anger. He is patient with us.

In Your Own Words

- As a human being, what benefits do you gain from God's slowness to anger?

- What does this example of God's slowness to anger mean for you as you seek to understand and control your anger? What do you learn from God about this?

∞

I like this statement from Lawrence Richards: "God's anger is always in harmony with his compassion, grace, love, faithfulness, eagerness to forgive, and commitment to do justice."[3] We *know* that God's slowness to anger is something He wants us to emulate because His Word teaches us exactly that: "Know this, my beloved brothers: let every person be quick to hear, slow to speak, *slow to anger;* for the anger of man does not produce the righteousness that God requires" (James 1:19-20).

In Your Own Words

- What reason does James give for not being quick-tempered?

∞

The blessing of being slow to anger—and the danger of being quick-tempered—is a frequent theme in the books of Proverbs and Ecclesiastes:

> A man of quick temper acts foolishly, and a man of evil devices is hated (Proverbs 14:17).

> Whoever is *slow to anger* has great understanding, but he who has a hasty temper exalts folly (14:29).

> Good sense makes one *slow to anger,* and it is his glory to overlook an offense (19:11).

> A fool gives full vent to his spirit, but a wise man quietly holds it back (29:11).

> Be not quick in your spirit to become angry, for anger lodges in the bosom of fools (Ecclesiastes 7:9).

In Your Own Words

⬡ According to the previous passages, what important contrasts should you keep in mind between "slow anger" and "quick temper"?

⬡

> A hot-tempered man stirs up strife, but he who is *slow to anger* quiets contention (Proverbs 15:18).

> A man of wrath stirs up strife, and one given to anger causes much transgression (29:22).

> Pressing milk produces curds, pressing the nose produces blood, and pressing anger produces strife (30:33).

In Your Own Words

⬡ In the previous verses, what connection do you see between anger and relational conflict?

- For the good of all our relationships, what is the value of being slow to anger?

> Whoever is *slow to anger* is better than the mighty, and he who rules his spirit than he who takes a city (Proverbs 16:32).

In Your Own Words

- Controlling your anger reflects true strength, doesn't it? And I think it *requires* true strength. Do you agree? Why or why not?

An Anger that Doesn't Last

Not only is God slow to anger, but His anger doesn't stay with Him as a controlling, dominant emotion. That's what David calls God's people to celebrate: "Sing praises to the LORD, O you his saints, and give thanks to his holy name. For *his anger is but for a moment,* and his favor is for a lifetime. Weeping may tarry for the night, but joy comes with the morning" (Psalm 30:4-5).

In Your Own Words

- What encouragement did that passage give you?

This is also what God communicated to His people through the prophet Jeremiah: "Return, faithless Israel, declares the LORD. I will not look on you in anger, for I am merciful, declares the LORD; *I will not be angry forever*" (Jeremiah 3:12). This encouraging truth is present as well when God expresses His loving promise to His people through the prophet Hosea: "How can I give you up, O Ephraim? How can I hand you over, O Israel?...My compassion grows warm and tender. *I will not execute my burning anger*…for I am God and not a man, the Holy One in your midst, and *I will not come in wrath*" (Hosea 11:8-9).

We see it also in the words of God spoken through Isaiah: "For my name's sake *I defer my anger,* for the sake of my praise I restrain it for you, that I may not cut you off" (Isaiah 48:9). And notice how this truth is pictured in this wonderfully rich passage, a promise made to the person who is "of a contrite and lowly spirit":

> "For *I will not contend forever, nor will I always be angry;* for the spirit would grow faint before me, and the breath of life that I made. Because of the iniquity of his unjust gain I was angry, I struck him; I hid my face and was angry, but he went on backsliding in the way of his own heart. I have seen his ways, but I will heal him; I will lead him and restore comfort to him and his mourners, creating the fruit of the lips. Peace, peace, to the far and to the near," says the LORD, "and I will heal him" (Isaiah 57:16-19).

In Your Own Words

⁜ How does that last passage from Isaiah reveal God's forbearance and compassion for His people in the way He exercises His anger toward them?

⁜ What is most significant to you in the way this passage portrays God's healing ways?

⟨∞⟩

In the Old Testament, when God's people were disobedient they did indeed see and experience the anger of God through rebuke and discipline. But many times they also saw and experienced this: "You forgave the iniquity of your people; you covered all their sin. *You withdrew all your wrath; you turned from your hot anger*" (Psalm 85:2-3).

As Lawrence Richards observes, "The Bible does not present

anger as an essential characteristic of God. In fact, God's wrath is set aside when God forgives, and even his acts of anger show restraint (Psalm 78:38). Compared to his favor, which lasts a lifetime, God's anger is momentary (Psalm 30:5). God intends only good to humanity, and when it is necessary to act in anger, the intention to do good is never lost."[4]

12

God's Love and Anger

In the pages of biblical prophecy describing God's anger with such power and passion, we also find passages that take us somewhere much higher, much better.

A New Start

The intense portrayal of God's anger in the book of Jeremiah serves to highlight all the more God's mercy and grace in the redemption He provides for His people. Jeremiah envisions a time when the Lord's wrath against His people will be over:

> Behold, I will gather them from all the countries to which I drove them *in my anger and my wrath and in great indignation.* I will bring them back to this place, and I will make them dwell in safety (Jeremiah 32:37).

The punishment God promised His people for their sins, and which He inflicted upon them in His anger, will be followed by the abundance of His upbuilding grace:

> And it shall come to pass that as I have watched over them to pluck up and break down, to overthrow, destroy, and bring harm, so I will watch over them to build and to plant, declares the LORD (Jeremiah 31:28).

And so there will come to God's people a fresh, new start—the new covenant we now enjoy and embrace through our Lord Jesus Christ, sealed by His blood:

> Behold, the days are coming, declares the LORD, when I will make a new covenant with the house of Israel and the house of Judah...I will put my law within them, and I will write it on their hearts. And I will be their God, and they shall be my people...They shall all know me, from the least of them to the greatest, declares the LORD. For I will forgive their iniquity, and I will remember their sin no more (31:31,33-34).

In Your Own Words

🔅 When you have a stronger view of God's anger toward His people's sin, how does that help you have a better understanding of God's new covenant and the redemption He gives us through Jesus and His forgiveness of your sins?

The Gospel and God's Anger

Because of the new start God's grace gives believers, the purpose of our lives here on earth is "to serve the living and true God, and to wait for his Son from heaven, whom he raised from the dead, *Jesus who delivers us from the wrath to come*" (1 Thessalonians 1:9-10). Hallelujah, Jesus!

Now we can *know*—in full assurance—that "God has not destined us for wrath, but to obtain salvation through our Lord Jesus Christ" (1 Thessalonians 5:9). As believers, our future will *not* include any taste from the cup of God's wrath. Jesus has ensured this for us by drinking that horrible cup Himself on our behalf—in His death on the cross. And He proved His triumph over death and sin by rising from the grave.

In Your Own Words

⬡ What does it mean for you, fully and personally, that Jesus delivered His people from the coming wrath of God?

⬡ What is your response to this in your heart and in your thoughts?

⬡

This wrath of God that we're delivered from is the ultimate consequence of the curse of sin and death that's been hanging over mankind. But now "Christ redeemed us from the curse of the law by becoming a curse for us" on the cross (Galatians 3:13).

"We all once lived in the passions of our flesh, carrying out the desires of the body and the mind, and were by nature *children of wrath*" (Ephesians 2:3). The glorious news is that Jesus on the cross absorbed all that wrath of God that was rightly coming to us. As Paul declares,

> Since, therefore, we have now been justified by his blood, *much more shall we be saved by him from the wrath of God.* For if while we were enemies we were reconciled to God by the death of his Son, much more, now that we are reconciled, shall we be saved by his life (Romans 5:9-10).

There cannot be any better news for us than that! I love these words from Lawrence Richards:

> Christ's self-sacrifice dealt so completely with sin that, as forgiven men and women, we are outside the sphere in which God's wrath operates. God does discipline believing men and women. But that discipline is totally an expression of love, not of anger (Hebrews 12:6).[1]

We're now "outside the sphere" of God's angry wrath. What freedom that gives us! What joy! And that's the central secret of how and why we can overcome our anger. In Romans 9:22-24, Paul presents a striking contrast that directly highlights God's wrath:

What if God, desiring to show *his wrath* and to make known his power, has endured with much patience *vessels of wrath* prepared for destruction, in order to make known the riches of his glory for vessels of mercy, which he has prepared beforehand for glory—even us whom he has called...?

In Your Own Words

❁ What is the difference between the "vessels of wrath" and the "vessels of mercy"?

❁ What is the wonderful thing God "makes known" to the vessels of mercy?

❁ What do you see as the most important truths this passage is teaching about God and His wrath as well as His mercy?

∞

Heavenly Father, I've learned so much about this hard-to-release condition of anger—this demon of oppression, this culprit of damaged feelings, this sinister controlling element in my mind and heart.

Now, Father, wash me white as snow as You forgive me for harboring anger and bitterness in my heart and mind. I repent of my disobedience and self-centeredness.

Help me hold fast to the teachings of Your Word and do my best to help others see Your truths in dealing with the horrors of anger.

In Jesus' name. Amen.

The Final End of God's Anger

Although the wrath of God came down on Jesus on the cross so that you and I, as believers, will never face God's wrath, there is another demonstration of God's anger that's coming up on His calendar. It's the day of final judgment on all those who choose not to believe and obey the Lord Jesus.

Here's a clarifying comment on this from Lawrence Richards:

> In the New Testament...the wrath of God is viewed as something that will come at the end of the age, not as something that operates in the present (except through such human agencies as government, Romans 13:4-5)... We are shown again and again in the New Testament that God's wrath is coming, not present. The time when God will again unleash his wrath is at history's end.[2]

This time is called "the day of the anger of the LORD" (see Zephaniah 2:1-2). "A day of wrath is that day, a day of distress and anguish, a day of ruin and devastation, a day of darkness and gloom, a day of clouds and thick darkness, a day of trumpet blast and battle cry" (Zephaniah 1:15-16).

Isaiah 63:1 gives us a picture of the Messiah on that day of final judgment, coming forth "in crimsoned garments...splendid in his apparel, marching in the greatness of his strength." And through Isaiah, the Lord says,

> It is I, speaking in righteousness, mighty to save...I have trodden the winepress alone, and from the peoples no one was with me; I trod them *in my anger* and trampled them *in my wrath*; their lifeblood spattered on my garments, and stained all my apparel. For the day of vengeance was in my heart, and my year of redemption had come. I looked, but there was no one to help; I was appalled, but there was no one to uphold; so my own arm brought me salvation, and *my wrath* upheld me. I trampled down the peoples *in my anger*; I made them drunk *in my wrath*, and I poured out their lifeblood on the earth" (Isaiah 63:1,3-6).

We get another picture of this at the end of the book of Isaiah:

> For behold, the LORD will come in fire, and his chariots like the whirlwind, to render his anger in fury, and his

rebuke with flames of fire. For by fire will the LORD enter into judgment, and by his sword, with all flesh; and those slain by the LORD shall be many (Isaiah 66:15-16).

In Your Own Words

❀ What stands out to you most in Isaiah's portrayal of God's anger in the final judgment?

❀ How do these passages help you better understand God's anger?

⌘

The New Testament clarifies this picture for us and emphasizes that when the day of final judgment comes—the day of God's wrath—that wrath will be directed toward those who refused to believe in Jesus Christ. A passage from one of Paul's letters echoes what we've seen in Isaiah. Paul tells of the day...

> when the Lord Jesus is revealed from heaven with his mighty angels *in flaming fire, inflicting vengeance* on those who do not know God and on those who do not obey the gospel of our Lord Jesus. They will suffer the punishment of eternal destruction, away from the presence of the Lord and from the glory of his might (2 Thessalonians 1:7-9).

In Your Own Words

❀ What does this passage teach you about God's anger, as reflected in Christ on the future day of judgment?

❀ How does this passage characterize those who will be subject to the Lord's anger on history's final day?

❀ Thinking of the unbelievers you know among your relatives and friends and neighbors and coworkers, how does this passage motivate you to share with them the truth of the gospel and the love of Jesus?

෨

This same truth is behind the following statement that we see in John's Gospel: "Whoever believes in the Son has eternal life; whoever does not obey the Son shall not see life, but *the wrath of God* remains on him" (John 3:36).

In Your Own Words

⚹ What does this verse teach you about God's anger?

⚹ What comes to your mind as you think about God's wrath "remaining" on someone?

෨

Meanwhile, for those who will not believe, their lack of faith is demonstrated by their disobedient actions. Paul tells us that the day is coming when "*the wrath of God* comes upon the sons of disobedience" (Ephesians 5:6). When he tells us to "put to death" such earthly behaviors as "sexual immorality, impurity, passion, evil desire, and covetousness," he immediately reminds us that "on account of these *the wrath of God* is coming" (Colossians 3:5-6).

Paul also tells us, "*The wrath of God* is revealed from heaven against all ungodliness and unrighteousness of men, who by their unrighteousness suppress the truth" (Romans 1:18). And he gives this warning to unbelievers: "Because of your hard and impenitent heart you are storing up *wrath* for yourself *on the day of wrath* when God's righteous judgment will be revealed" (Romans 2:5). Paul then passes along this promise from God about the eternal future: "For those who are self-seeking and do not obey the truth, but obey unrighteousness, there will be *wrath and fury*" (Romans 2:8).

In Your Own Words

✽ How would you summarize what these scriptures from Paul teach about God's anger?

⊜

God's wrath is being stored up for those who are stubbornly unrepentant. Meanwhile, "in regard to unbelievers, God graciously is holding back expression of deserved wrath, to give everyone opportunity for repentance. Those who will not respond to grace store up wrath, a wrath to be experienced in the day of final judgment."[3]

As the forerunner to the ministry of Jesus, John the Baptist powerfully warned of "the wrath to come" (see Matthew 3:7; Luke 3:7). And when we turn to the end of the New Testament, we find God's coming wrath shown in intense and unforgettable pictures in the book of Revelation. We see people "calling to the mountains and rocks, 'Fall on us and hide us from the face of him who is seated on the throne, and from *the wrath of the Lamb,* for *the great day of their wrath has come, and who can stand?*'" (Revelation 6:16-17).

We also see the 24 elders falling on their faces and saying to God, "The nations raged, but *your wrath came,* and the time for the dead to be judged, and for rewarding your servants, the prophets and saints, and those who fear your name, both small and great, and for destroying the destroyers of the earth" (11:18).

We hear an angel crying out,

> If anyone worships the beast and its image and receives a mark on his forehead or on his hand, he also will drink the *wine of God's wrath,* poured full strength into *the cup of his anger,* and he will be tormented with fire and sulfur in the presence of the holy angels and in the presence of the Lamb. And the smoke of their torment goes up forever and ever, and they have no rest, day or night, these worshipers of the beast and its image, and whoever receives the mark of its name (14:9-11).

We watch as an angel comes out of God's temple in heaven, carrying a sharp sickle, ready to harvest the earth.

> And another angel came out from the altar, the angel who has authority over the fire, and he called with a loud voice to the one who had the sharp sickle, "Put in your sickle and gather the clusters from the vine of the earth, for its grapes are ripe." So the angel swung his sickle across the earth and gathered the grape harvest of the earth and threw it into *the great winepress of the wrath of God* (14:18-19).

We see seven angels coming out of the heavenly sanctuary, and they are given "seven golden bowls *full of the wrath of God* who lives forever and ever" (15:7). Then from God's heavenly temple we a hear a shout of command given to these angels: "Go and pour out on the earth the seven bowls of *the wrath of God*" (16:1). And when all seven of those bowls of wrath are poured out, we witness the power of Satan's mightiest strongholds broken: "The cities of the nations fell, and God remembered Babylon the great, to make her drain the cup of the wine of the fury of his wrath" (16:19).

And then comes perhaps the mightiest image of all, the ultimate picture of righteous wrath conquering all evil. We see heaven opened…

> And behold, a white horse! The one sitting on it is called Faithful and True, and in righteousness he judges and makes war. His eyes are like a flame of fire, and on his head are many diadems, and he has a name written that no one knows but himself. He is clothed in a robe dipped in blood, and the name by which he is called is The Word of God. And the armies of heaven, arrayed in fine linen, white and pure, were following him on white horses. From his mouth comes a sharp sword with which to strike down the nations, and he will rule them with a rod of iron. He will tread the winepress of *the fury of the wrath of God the Almighty*. On his robe and on his thigh he has a name written, King of kings and Lord of lords (Revelation 19:11-16).

In Your Own Words

❊ What do these images from Revelation teach you about the righteous anger of God?

❊ What stands out to you most in these passages?

∞

There was a time when "we all once lived in the passions of our flesh, carrying out the desires of the body and the mind, and were by nature *children of wrath*, like the rest of mankind" (Ephesians 2:3). But the amazing, glorious good news is that Jesus on the cross absorbed all that wrath of God that was rightly coming to us. As Paul declares,

> Since, therefore, we have now been justified by his blood, *much more shall we be saved by him from the wrath of God.* For if while we were enemies we were reconciled to God by the death of his Son, much more, now that we are reconciled, shall we be saved by his life (Romans 5:9-10).

There isn't any better news for us than that!

This is my prayer, Lord, that I will always remember the effects of good and bad anger. I pray I will never sin in anger and the night will never overshadow my obedience to Your Word. I pray that anger will become a "has been," not a "still here" situation for me. And if I fail You, Lord, please hear my contrite heart and forgive me. I ask this in Jesus' name. Amen.

13

Victory over Anger

My husband, George, and I have been married for 50 years, and a fifth of that time was saturated with anger in some shape, form, or fashion. We got tired of it and made a promise that we've kept all these years.

I entered marriage with the idea that we would live happily ever after. I thought we would never disagree, and that each of us was all the other needed in the world. Looking back, I now know I was looking at him as my idol. He did not have the same sense of idolatry toward me. Yes, he loved me, but he was more realistic than I was. And I could sense that. So for about 15 years I was determined to "mold him in *my* image" and make him exactly what I thought I wanted in a man and husband. It never worked! But I wouldn't give up my campaign to bring him to perfection. This kept strife and tension brewing a lot of the time.

Because he wouldn't acquiesce to my wants and desires, I was angry. I began to think he didn't really love me (even though he showed me his love all the time). I was provoked. And all of *his* faults stuck out like a sore thumb.

I got so tired of arguing, so tired of feeling depressed, angry, and abandoned in my mind. And my husband got tired of the havoc in our lives. So he asked me to join with him in a truce in which we would promise each other never again to go to sleep feeling anger toward each other. I reluctantly agreed.

Meanwhile, during that same time of being fatigued by the stress and clamor of our lives, I began studying my Bible again, asking God to show me where I was wrong. I also began talking to a godly woman and confiding in her about the turmoil I was experiencing. I started listening to wisdom from her and others, and began to look critically and intentionally at my role in my marriage.

And oh, thank God, I went to Christian counseling for help. I went by myself and without anyone's knowledge. And through the counsel of God I saw that it was my low self-esteem and my unrealistic expectations that were the culprits. Sure, my husband had some issues, but I learned that he was not responsible for my emotional well-being. That was *my* responsibility. I learned that God had made both my husband and me with personality and DNA that are individual and unique to each of us. I learned that I, as my husband's helpmeet, was designed and equipped by God to build him up, to bless him, and to love him unconditionally as God loves me. I learned that I needed to appreciate what he had done all those years by enduring my nagging attempts to change him. I learned to get over my self-centeredness and to be sensitive to the man of my love and life who had never changed in his love for me and who was ever faithful to me.

Through faith in God and trust in His Word, through gaining help from other Christians who had wise counsel, and through my desire to change my life (and our marriage) for the better, I worked diligently to see me as God does...to love my husband as God loves me...to admit to George my insensitivities...and to submit myself to the mighty hand of God. I endeavored to return to my first love—the Lord Himself—who was going to restore George's and my love and marriage so I could live as bone of his bone and flesh of his flesh.

To seal the deal, we stood before a minister on Christian television and rededicated ourselves to living our lives together as God commanded. That same Sunday, I stood before the altar of God in our church, and during the intercessory prayer gave myself and my feelings totally God—and He washed me clean.

Have we had conflicts since that time? Of course we have. But we have learned to agree to disagree and to never carry over any hurt, shame, guilt, or any other divisive thing into another day.

From that time to this, we have never gone to sleep being angry with each other. We've had some sleepless nights—but before the night ends, one of us will be humble to the other, and we will discuss the situation, pray together, and forgive each other. Once we extend that forgiveness, there's no need to bring up the offense again if we have truly forgiven each other.

We do not live in anger. We're free to be ourselves and free to allow the other to be him- or herself unconditionally.

Oh what freedom from anger! And I've learned to experience this freedom from anger not only toward my husband, but also toward everyone I meet. This doesn't mean I don't get angry, but it does mean that I know how God requires me to handle the temptation to be angry before Him. I try to do that quickly, and to not waste time with things that are not mine to fix, bear, hold on to, dominate, manipulate, direct, or overthrow. I cast it all on Him who is able to do all things well.

And when necessary, I'm determined to get angry—yes, to get angry at sin. But I'm also determined not be a victim of sin myself. I understand that all the battles we fight in life are not ours to fight if we are God's children. *The battle belongs to the Lord!*

You too can become angry at the appropriate things to be mad about, but as far as sinning with your anger, God has given you a means of escape:

> The temptations in your life are no different from what others experience. And God is faithful. He will not allow the temptation to be more than you can stand. When you are tempted, he will show you a way out so that you can endure (1 Corinthians 10:13 NLT).

Steps to Victory

Anger is such a common problem and snare for so many—yet we

are fortunate that so many pastors and mentors and Bible teachers and counselors are faithful to offer encouragement and help on this issue as they learn more about it themselves.

Following are the steps to victory that Pastor Bob Mutch offers in his personal blog. I think there is a great deal here that can be helpful for us.

1. *Attitude change.* You must change your attitude towards whatever degree of anger you are dealing with in your life. You must reject the idea that this is a weakness or a sin that you will have to bear for the rest of your life, or you will not be able to get victory over it.

There is power in the name of Jesus to deliver and keep you from all sin and help you in "perfecting holiness in the fear of God" (2 Corinthians 7:1 NASB). "God is able to make all grace abound to you" (2 Corinthians 9:8), and to help you grow in patience and meekness and have greater victory in your life...

Also, it is important to not overlook your conduct just because it may only happen once in a while. The Christian graces you have are only as high as they are at your worse moment. You are only as spiritual as you are in your lowest conduct. What comes out of your life in the middle of your worst trial is what was there all along.

2. *Flee to Christ.* Whenever you start to feel irritated, frustrated, or annoyed, you must stop everything you are doing and go and pray. If you are at work, you should go and take a restroom break and pray there. Pray until you have the victory over these feelings.

You may need to take a break from what you are doing and come back to it later if you find the task annoying. The reason Christians get upset or angry is because they do not go to prayer and seek God for help, but keep on going in their own strength. This is where failure comes in.

3. *Hear and follow the voice of God.* You must learn to listen and hear the voice of God. He will be faithful to warn

you that temptation is on its way and that you need to pray. You must make it a matter of prayer every day that God will help you to hear His quiet voice of warning. Then, when you hear it, you must heed it. How many times have you gotten into trouble by overriding the voice of the Lord?

4. *Increase your faith through prayer and the Word.* Anytime you have a lack in your Christian walk, you need more grace and faith. By reading the Word of God and seeking God in prayer, your faith will be increased.

You build faith by hearing the Word of God (Romans 10:17), and by praying in the Holy Spirit (Jude 20). It is by faith that you stand (2 Corinthians 1:24; Romans 11:20), by faith that you have victory over the world (1 John 5:4), by faith that you quench all the fiery darts of the wicked one (Ephesians 6:16), and through faith you are being guarded by the power of God from sin (1 Peter 1:5).

5. *Confession.* Any actions of anger that you have expressed towards another person needs to be confessed first to God, and then to the person you expressed them toward. Immediately, when you realize you have acted in a way that is below the Gospel standard, go and pray and ask God to help you, empower you, and forgive you.

Pray until the feelings of anger go away. Cry out to God and plead the blood of Jesus. Then go to the person and humble yourself, taking all blame to yourself, and confess and ask for forgiveness. If they are a Christian, it may be in order to ask them to pray with you and for you. Let them know you take these things seriously and that you are looking to Jesus for complete victory.

When you humble yourself in this way, the Word of God promises grace. "God resisteth the proud, but giveth grace unto the humble" (James 4:6 KJV). A commitment to ask others for forgiveness brings with it a shame factor that also helps you resist wrong attitudes and conduct.[1]

A.N.G.E.R.

Here are more encouraging words about victory over anger from author and retired corporate executive Linda Law:

> Anger is a reality in everyone's life! There are some who have short fuses and blow up; others can't deal with the anger so they hold it in and allow it to grow.
>
> God wants you to be victorious (1 Corinthians 10:12-13) *before* the problem of anger presents itself. He has given you the way out, the way to be victorious and to guard against Satan seeking to defeat you. Have faith by thanking Him for your victory (Philippians 4:13; Luke 1:37; 1 Corinthians 15:57). If you believe you have failed, go to 1 John 1:8; 1 John 2:2.
>
> When you are "unforgiving," you are one moment away from being angry and depressed. Thus…you give the person you will not forgive complete power and control over *you*! Humble yourself (Romans 12:3), and recognize that you are the steward of the blessings that God has given you. Choosing to not forgive is a form of rebellion against God (Psalm 51:4; 1 John 1:9).
>
> Be faithful in studying God's Word, in order to allow God to live within you and change your wrong thinking. Be a good communicator by listening carefully; then speak only those words that you can say that are truly spoken with love. You are in control of a dangerous weapon… your mouth! (James 2:1-12; Proverbs 8:8; 15:1).
>
> Total commitment to the right conviction will bring about success and change (2 Corinthians 5:17). Living positive is an ongoing process, and it becomes a continuation of ridding negative thinking and replacing it with God's thinking from the Word of God.
>
> *ANGER* (ways people justify negative actions!):
>
> > (A) *Attitude.* When you are attacked, attack back! "Everybody does it."

(**N**) *Negative.* "Nothing ever goes right."

(**G**) *Guilt.* Being bitter and resentful always brings anger!

(**E**) *Emotion.* Emotions are out of control when you refuse to allow your brain to do what it should!

(**R**) *Rejection.* Being rejected by others...not being accepted by them.

As you read those words attached to ANGER as listed...it becomes apparent that *you* have *decided to get angry*! When you rationalize it by thinking, *Other people irritate me, frustrate and aggravate me, so I get angry!*— have you stopped to realize that *you* decided to get angry? The other person/situation did not *make* you choose anger; you chose it! Victory over anger begins by being account-able for your actions (Romans 14:12)...

We ultimately choose our goal in life—my hope is that you will give this subject more serious thought, begin a plan to study the Word in order to be better prepared; and also to make a commitment for yourself. Commit your-self to be spiritual, to allow God's will and words to resolve conflicts. Glorify God by bearing fruit, involving your-self in positive works; avoid and resolve conflict in positive ways; and speak in the positive, allowing that resolution to be in your future...

You can control anger and turn it into Positive! You are the master of your own mouth...use it in a way that will bring goodness into your life! Seek harmony and peace, and encourage others through your kind words; it will amaze you how quickly your own life will change for the better![2]

Victory Through Forgiving Others

I've talked a lot in this book about the vital importance of forgiving others who have caused our anger. That's something we must always remember. The continued practice of forgiveness toward others will speed us down the path of victory over anger.

Do you know people who refuse to forgive? If so, you've probably noticed that unforgiveness causes family members to be at odds with each other, negatively impacts marriages and personal relationships, often results in job difficulties or getting fired, and even brings about serious illnesses because of the poisonous venom of holding on to hurts and disappointments.

The grudges and hatred (yes, hatred) they hold against people, I believe, often stem from the disappointments and despair they have of themselves for not realizing the successes they could have had, disappointing their families, and blaming other people for their bad choices. They are often jealous of the successes of others and believe people are making fun or ridiculing them. Sometimes these people have even forgotten the details of why they haven't forgiven! They just continue in their habitual anger.

There is an answer even for people hardened with anger. Jesus! If they'll turn to Him and give Him all their disappointments, hurts, anger, and pain...if they'll accept Him as their Savior and follow Him, He will heal their woundedness and give them hope! And just think what a new life they will have if they discover how to forgive in Jesus!

Look what people get when they decide to forgive. (It is a decision, you know.) We become healthier physically. Forgiveness is an antidote for worry, anxiety, depression, and phobias. Relationships become easier. Forgiveness takes responsibility for our emotional stability off other people. It gives back our sense of stability and adjusts our longing for association. The seat of our existence becomes consistent with our spirit. When our mind, soul, and spirit are consistent we are able to think more clearly, be more loving and compassionate, and experience greater intimacy with God.

Why not take a hard look at yourself? Ask if you are holding a grudge against anyone—including yourself. If you are, evaluate the situation. Is holding a grudge producing anything positive? Is it blocking any goodwill? Is it hindering loving people, God, or yourself? How do you think you would feel if you totally surrendered your feelings of hatred or lack of forgiveness to God? Right now, sugar, this is all about you. What would your life look like without the negativity?

Now figure out what you need to do to erase the hard feelings. Here are several steps to forgiveness that I have seen work:

- Admit you are holding a grudge or hatred in your heart.

- Ask God to forgive you and allow Him to wash His love over your spirit.

- Praise God for His work of forgiving in your life.

- Ask God to help you want to forgive. (Yes, sometimes we just don't want to.)

- With God's help, *choose to forgive.*

- Tell the person(s) you forgive him or her. If the person is no longer available or it would be dangerous to contact him or her, express out loud that you forgive them and act accordingly.

Now, let me emphasize what you will discover now that you've forgiven!

- Your joy will be restored.

- Your health can be improved.

- Your hopes will increase.

- Your dreams will began to materialize.

- Your smile will return, along with the twinkle in your eyes.

- Your song will begin to resound.

- Your friendships and relationships will blossom.

- Your nights will be more restful.

- Your laughter will return.

- Your life will gain renewed significance.

- Your heart will beat with increased love.

How do I know? I've lived it! I've seen those who forgive make refreshing U-turns in their lives and enjoy the sweet nectar of a fresh, new season.

Forgiveness Is an Antidote for Anger

Wendell Miller, the cofounder and executive director of the Biblical Counseling Association, in his book *Forgiveness: The Power and the Puzzles,* speaks about the power of forgiveness as the antidote for anger. I'd like you to hear the following wise words from him, especially as he discusses Ephesians 4:31-32: "Let all bitterness and wrath and anger and clamor and slander be put away from you, along with all malice. And be kind to one another, tender-hearted, forgiving each other, just as God in Christ also has forgiven you."[3]

> Understanding the conjunction "and" that connects Ephesians 4:31 and 4:32 is helpful in gaining an understanding of *God's antidote for anger.* This "and" in the Greek New Testament is not like "Jack and Jill went up the hill"—it does not connect two things in parallel. Instead, it shows a sequential, causal, or consequential relationship between two ideas, thoughts, or actions.
>
> Sometimes this "and" is translated "that is" to introduce an explanation. If we translate this "and" with "that is," then verses 31 and 32, paraphrased, say, "Let God put away your bad feelings. That is, do what verse 32 teaches."
>
> Verse 32 says that the way to "let God" put away your anger, is to forgive. But how are you to forgive?… "as God…has forgiven you"…
>
> If we are to forgive "as God has forgiven us," then, even as God's repetitive judicial forgiveness of us, as believers, is unconditional, we must forgive unconditionally. We must forgive anytime we have anything against anyone (Mark 11:25). We cannot, we must not, wait for repentance of those who offend us (Luke 17:3-4).
>
> So what is God's antidote for bitterness, wrath, and anger? *Forgiveness.* Pray and release the penalty of the

offense to God if/whenever you have anything against anyone, as taught in Mark 11:25.[4]

In just a couple of verses in Psalm 37, we find a comprehensive program for dealing with our anger as it occurs, especially when that anger is provoked by the wrongdoing of other people:

> Be still before the LORD and wait patiently for him; fret not yourself over the one who prospers in his way, over the man who carries out evil devices! Refrain from anger, and forsake wrath! Fret not yourself; it tends only to evil. For the evildoers shall be cut off, but those who wait for the LORD shall inherit the land (verses 7-9).

In Your Own Words

❧ How would you summarize the best ways to deal with anger, according to what we see in these verses from Psalm 37?

❧ How does this passage reinforce your personal responsibility for how you deal with your anger?

∞

Lawrence Richards says rightly that we need to share all our emotions—how we're feeling—with God:

> When we are angry, we are to accept the fact that we are angry and to express those feelings to God...In expressing our feelings to God we consciously relate our situation to him and thus change our perception of it...When we remember that God rules the world of people, peace will come as we turn our situation over to him.[5]

Psalm 37 reveals God's prescription for handling anger and frustration: Give them to Him. We're to...

let the realization of who God is reshape our perspective and reshape our emotions as well...A person may not be able to prevent a sudden rush of angry feelings. But each of us can choose to turn from the course that anger suggests. We can choose not to harbor anger and not to do the evil that anger urges us to do. We can rest our hope instead in the Lord.[6]

Dealing with Angry People

Do you ever encounter angry people? I'm sure you do. There are plenty of them out there! So how should we respond to them? Here's one thing to remember: "Make no friendship with a man given to anger, nor go with a wrathful man, lest you learn his ways and entangle yourself in a snare" (Proverbs 22:24-25).

In Your Own Words

❀ Have you considered that a tendency to anger can "rub off" from one person to another?

❀ Have you seen this happen in your life? Explain.

❀ What do you think is the most appropriate way to apply these verses from Proverbs 22 to your life?

∞

Here's an interesting perspective on involvement with angry people: "A man of great wrath will pay the penalty, for if you deliver him, you will only have to do it again" (Proverbs 19:19).

In Your Own Words

❀ What kind of "penalties" have you seen angry people having to pay?

❧ Describe a time or two when you've seen angry people who don't seem to learn from the consequences of their outbursts.

❧ What do you think is the most appropriate way to apply Proverbs 19:19 to your life?

14

From Anger to Peace

If you've been angry in life as I have, and you have come to the point of releasing that anger, as I have, then something wonderful will happen. When you give that anger to God, when you release to Him the people who have hurt you and who have triggered your anger, then His peace comes into your heart and in your spirit in ways we humans can't understand. This peace is talked about in Philippians 4:6-7:

> Do not be anxious about anything, but in everything by prayer and supplication with thanksgiving let your requests be made known to God. And *the peace of God, which surpasses all understanding,* will guard your hearts and your minds in Christ Jesus.

We're told not to worry about a thing! Instead we are to pray about anything that might be disturbing us and place that situation into the capable hands of God, who will take care of if for us. And we do this "with thanksgiving"—being grateful that God solves every problem, takes care of every situation, and never leaves us. Before the world began, our loving God already took care of the situations we face. Isn't that wonderful! And we can give Him thanks that the results of everything going on in our lives, including those things we get angry about—have been planned, designed, covered by His love and mercy, and wrapped up in a package of His grace and provision for our lives.

As Philippians 4 says, "Let your requests be made known to God." Bring your petitions before Him!

My petition is that I will never feel out-of-control, unrighteous anger again as I have in the past.

My petition to God is that victory will be mine in every situation as I draw on His strength and wisdom. As I expressed through the title of one of my books: *Don't give in…God wants you to win!*

And that means, as I said in another book title, being *ready to win over worry and anxiety.* And yes, as I said in another one, it means being *ready to win over depression* too. Those states can all be closely linked to the anger urges we so often feel.

But let's also be ready to win over our selfish motives. Let's be ready to win over our failure to forgive. True, people may not deserve to be forgiven, but that doesn't matter. We're *commanded* to forgive. Forgiveness of others is easier when we think of all we have done—all the people we have let down and hurt—that we depend on God to forgive us for. And when we think how we've sinned against Him—how we've done little things and big things that are contrary to His will—and how much and often He continues to forgive us, we can keep growing in our ability to extend His loving grace and forgiveness to others as well.

Now, when it comes to extending forgiveness, sometimes people who have harmed us never ask to be forgiven. But remember, we live under the dispensation of grace. *Grace is unmerited favor.* We don't deserve it, never will deserve it, but God gives it anyway, along with mercy, forgiveness, love. And that's where we should live every day, every minute—on Love Street with Him.

On Love Street, we will not hold on to the things that bring us anger. We will not harbor grudges. Bitterness will not be part of our addresses. On Love Street we will do to others even better than we want them to do for us.

Anger is a sin when we hold on to it—when we allow it to hurt people and us. And when we are disobedient to God's will to forgive—that's sin.

But when we release that hurt that we're holding on to, oh, what joy! What *joy!* Thank You, Lord! What joy! And this joy leaves no opening for anger, no room for rage, no freedom for fury.

> *Jesus, in the name of the Father and the Son and the Holy Spirit, we thank You! Amen!*

Words of Peace

Let me conclude with God's words of promise about the peace He bestows, the peace that makes our anger disappear. I hope you will reflect deeply on these encouraging words and return here often to guard you from anger's destructive fires:

> Peace I leave with you; my peace I give to you. Not as the world gives do I give to you. Let not your hearts be troubled, neither let them be afraid (John 14:27).

> Therefore, since we have been justified by faith, we have peace with God through our Lord Jesus Christ (Romans 5:1).

> But he was wounded for our transgressions; he was crushed for our iniquities; upon him was the chastisement that brought us peace, and with his stripes we are healed (Isaiah 53:5).

> Now may the Lord of peace himself give you peace at all times in every way. The Lord be with you all (2 Thessalonians 3:16).

> You keep him in perfect peace whose mind is stayed on you, because he trusts in you (Isaiah 26:3).

> Turn away from evil and do good; seek peace and pursue it (Psalm 34:14).

> And let the peace of Christ rule in your hearts, to which

indeed you were called in one body. And be thankful (Colossians 3:15).

And the peace of God, which surpasses all understanding, will guard your hearts and your minds in Christ Jesus (Philippians 4:7).

The LORD make his face to shine upon you and be gracious to you; the LORD lift up his countenance upon you and give you peace (Numbers 6:25-26).

Pray for the peace of Jerusalem! "May they be secure who love you!" (Psalm 122:6).

He makes peace in your borders; he fills you with the finest of the wheat (Psalm 147:14).

If possible, so far as it depends on you, live peaceably with all (Romans 12:18).

Great peace have those who love your law; nothing can make them stumble (Psalm 119:165).

But the fruit of the Spirit is love, joy, peace, patience, kindness, goodness, faithfulness... (Galatians 5:22).

In peace I will both lie down and sleep; for you alone, O LORD, make me dwell in safety (Psalm 4:8).

When a man's ways please the LORD, he makes even his enemies to be at peace with him (Proverbs 16:7).

And the effect of righteousness will be peace, and the result of righteousness, quietness and trust forever (Isaiah 32:17).

I have said these things to you, that in me you may have peace. In the world you will have tribulation. But take heart; I have overcome the world (John 16:33).

May the LORD give strength to his people! May the LORD bless his people with peace! (Psalm 29:11).

May the God of hope fill you with all joy and peace in believing, so that by the power of the Holy Spirit you may abound in hope (Romans 15:13).

In Your Own Words

❈ Which verses in this list of encouraging scriptures mean the most for you right now?

❈ What are the most important things you've learned from this book?

The Essence of Victory over Anger

The essence of victory over anger lies in a word we really don't like to hear: *submission*. That is, *submission to the will of God*. If you don't like the word *submission*, let's use *surrender* to the will of God.

I can't complete this work on anger without singing a song of surrender and thanking God for the opportunity to accept victory over anger. Let's sing "I Surrender All" together!

> All to Jesus, I surrender;
> All to Him I freely give;
> I will ever love and trust Him,
> In His presence daily live.
>
> I surrender all,
> I surrender all,
> All to Thee, my blessed Savior,
> I surrender all.
>
> All to Jesus I surrender;
> Humbly at His feet I bow,
> Worldly pleasures all forsaken;
> Take me, Jesus, take me now.

All to Jesus, I surrender;
Make me, Savior, wholly Thine;
Let me feel the Holy Spirit,
Truly know that Thou art mine.

All to Jesus, I surrender;
Lord, I give myself to Thee;
Fill me with Thy love and power;
Let Thy blessing fall on me.

All to Jesus, I surrender;
Now I feel the sacred flame.
O the joy of full salvation!
Glory, glory, to His Name![1]

I surrender all,
I surrender all,
All to Thee, my blessed Savior,
I surrender all.

Notes

Chapter 1: This Thing Called Anger

1. The Free Dictionary, accessed April 16, 2011, http://www.thefreedictionary.com, s.v. anger.

2. Wikipedia, accessed April 16, 2011, https://secure.wikimedia.org/wikipedia/en/wiki/, s.v. anger.

3. Thomas Aquinas, *The Summa Theologica* (Benziger Bros. ed., 1947), trans. by Fathers of the English Dominican Province, "First part of the second part (qq. 1-114); 'Of Anger, in Itself' (eight articles)." Accessed April 5, 2011, http://www.ccel.org/a/aquinas/summa/FS.html.

4. Information in this chapter about the Hebrew and Greek words used for *anger* in Scripture is adapted primarily from Lawrence O. Richards, "Anger," *Zondervan Expository Dictionary of Bible Words* (Grand Rapids, MI: Zondervan, 1991), pp. 46-51; and from H. Schonweiss and H.C. Hahn, "Anger," *The New International Dictionary of New Testament Theology*, Colin Brown, gen. ed. (Grand Rapids, MI: Zondervan, 1975), vol. 1, 105-13.

5. Lawrence O. Richards, "Anger," *Zondervan Expository Dictionary of Bible Words* (Grand Rapids, MI: Zondervan, 1991), 46.

Chapter 2: Causes, Trigger Points, and Warning Signs

1. Adapted from Doug Britton, "What Makes You Angry," © 2001, 2007 by Doug Britton, adapted from his book *Victory over Grumpiness, Irritation, and Anger* (North Highlands, CA: BibleSource Publications, 2004), accessed April 14, 2011, http://www.dougbrittonbooks.com/onlinebiblestudies-irritationandangermanagement/anger-identifyreasonsyouareangry.php. Used by permission.

2. Harry Mills, PhD, "Recognizing Anger Signs," accessed April 17, 2011, http://www.mentalhelp.net/poc/view_doc.php?type=doc&id=5812.

3. Diane Eaton, "Anger—A Dangerous Weapon," ch. 1, in "Why Are You Angry?" at the website The WayBack.net, accessed April 22, 2011, http://www.quiteexcellent.com/thewayback.net/articles/ANGER/1weapon.htm, copyright © 2002 TheWayBack.net by Diane Eaton. Used by permission.

Chapter 3: Good Anger?

1. Matthew Henry, *Matthew Henry Complete Commentary on the Whole Bible*, accessed April 20, 2011, http://www.studylight.org/com/mhc-com/view.cgi?book=eph&chapter=004.

2. NIV Study Bible (Grand Rapids, MI: Zondervan, 1985), Ephesians 4:26-27.

3. Life Application Bible (Wheaton, IL: Tyndale, 1988), Ephesians 4:26-27.

4. ESV Study Bible (Wheaton, IL: Crossway, 2008), Ephesians 4:26-27.

5. Eaton, "Anger—A Dangerous Weapon," accessed April 22, 2011. Used by permission.

6. Douglas L. Rutt, "Lutheran Missiology" blog, comments on Matthew 9:2-13 and quoting Matthew 9:12, accessed April 23, 2011, http://www.lutheranmissiology.org/Matt9.pdf.

Chapter 4: Angry at God?

1. Quest Study Bible, Phyllis Ten Elshof, gen. ed. (Grand Rapids, MI: Zondervan, 2003), Job 15.

2. John Piper, "Is It Ever Right to Be Angry at God?," © Desiring God, accessed April 16, 2011, http://www.desiringgod.org/resource-library/taste-see-articles/is-it-ever-right-to-be-angry-at-god.

3. Doug Britton, "Is It a Sin to Be Angry with God?" © 2007 Doug Britton, accessed April 16, 2011, http://www.dougbrittonbooks.com/onlinebiblestudies-irritationandangermanagement/angrywithgod.php. Used by permission.

4. Randy Alcorn, *If God Is Good* (Colorado Springs: Multnomah, 2009), 218-19.

Chapter 5: Anger and Our Children

1. Ross Campbell with Rob Suggs, *How to Really Love Your Angry Child* (Colorado Springs: Cook Communications, 1995), 110.

2. Ron Rhodes, "Teaching Kids to Control Anger," accessed April 16, 2011, http://christianparentingcenter.com/christian_parenting_advice_teach_kids_to_control_anger.html. Used by permission.

3. Michele Borba, "Six Ways to Help Kids Handle Anger," adapted from *Parents Do Make a Difference: How to Raise Kids with Solid Character, Strong Minds, and Caring Hearts* (San Francisco: Jossey-Bass, 1999); © 1999 by Michele Borba, accessed April 17, 2011, http://www.parentingbookmark.com/pages/articleMB01.htm.

Chapter 6: Anger Management

1. Adapted from Reachout.com, accessed April 10, 2011, http://au.reachout.com/find/articles/anger.

Chapter 7: More Help for Controlling Anger

1. The Yahshua Institute, "Be Angry and Sin Not: Bible Teaching About Controlling Your Temper and Anger," accessed April 11, 2011, https://theoraclemag.wordpress.com/2009/04/28/be-angry-and-sin-not-bible-teaching-about-controlling-your-temper-and-anger/.

2. From "Are You Angry? Dealing with Anger according to the Bible" at the "ShareFaith" website, accessed April 13, 2011, http://www.sharefaithblog.com/2010/09/angry-dealing-anger-bible/#more-1350.

Chapter 8: Anger's Harmful Effects

1. Tyler Woods, "The Effect of Anger," accessed April 24, 2011, http://www.angelfire.com/mo/countrysoulcafe/anger.html.

2. Katherine Kam, "How Anger Hurts Your Heart," WebMD, accessed April 23, 2011, http://www.webmd.com/balance/stress-management/features/how-anger-hurts-your-heart.

Chapter 9: What God's Word Teaches About Anger

1. Richards, "Anger," *Zondervan Expository Dictionary*, 47.
2. ESV Study Bible (Wheaton, IL: Crossway, 2008), Exodus 11:8.
3. Richards, "Anger," *Zondervan Expository Dictionary*, 50.

Chapter 11: Observing God's Anger

1. Richards, "Anger," *Zondervan Expository Dictionary*, 48.
2. Ibid., 49.
3. Ibid.
4. Ibid.

Chapter 12: God's Love and Anger

1. Richards, "Anger," *Zondervan Expository Dictionary*, 50.
2. Ibid.
3. Ibid., 51.

Chapter 13: Victory over Anger

1. Bob Mutch, "More Christ Like" personal blog, accessed April 17, 2011, http://morechristlike.com/victory-over-anger/. Used by permission. Mutch is a pastor in Ontario, Canada.
2. Linda Law, "Victory over Anger"; accessed April 12, 2011, http://www.authorsden.com/visit/viewArticle.asp?id=46952, adapted. Used by permission.
3. Ephesians 4:31-32, New American Standard Bible®, © 1960, 1962, 1963, 1968, 1971, 1972, 1973, 1975, 1977 by The Lockman Foundation, www.Lockman.org.
4. Wendell E. Miller, *Forgiveness: The Power and the Puzzles* (Warsaw, Indiana: ClearBrook Publishers, 1997), accessed April 23, 2011, http://www.biblical-counsel.org/forg-ang.htm.
5. Richards, "Anger," *Zondervan Expository Dictionary*, 48.
6. Ibid.

Chapter 14: From Anger to Peace

1. "I Surrender All," words by Judson W. Van DeVenter, 1896.

About the Author

THELMA WELLS' life has been a courageous journey of faith. Born to an unwed and physically disabled teenager, the name on Thelma's birth certificate read simply "Baby Girl Morris." Her mother worked as a maid in the "big house" while they lived in the servants' quarters. When Thelma stayed at her grandparents' home, her mentally ill grandmother locked her in a dark, smelly, insect-infested closet all day. To ease her fear, Thelma sang every hymn and praise song she knew.

A trailblazer for black women, Thelma worked in the banking industry and was a professor at Master's International School of Divinity. Her vivacious personality and talent for storytelling attracted the attention of the Women of Faith Tour. She was soon one of their core speakers. She was named Extraordinary Woman of the Year in 2008 by the Extraordinary Women Conferences. She also received the Advanced Writers and Speakers Association's Lifetime Achievement Award in 2009.

Along with writing books, including *Don't Give In...God Wants You to Win!* Thelma is president of Woman of God Ministries. "Mama T," as she is affectionately called, helps girls and women all over the world discover Jesus and live for Him.

Thelma earned degrees at North Texas State University and Master's International School of Divinity. She was awarded an honorary PhD from St. Thomas Christian College and Theological Seminary and ordained through the Association of Christian Churches in Florida.

Thelma and George, her husband of 48 years, enjoy spending time with their children, grandchildren, and great-grandchildren.

∞

For more information about Thelma and her ministry, check out
www.thelmawells.com

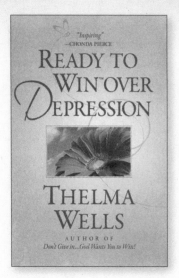

You don't have to feel good or positive to start this book.

You are not alone or crazy.

You can start winning over depression today!

Has sadness taken over? Have you talked, prayed, and even focused on "happy thoughts" but continue to slog through every day? Popular author Thelma Wells has been there. She knows it's hard to start down the recovery road, but she did...and reached the promised land of hope and joy. And she wants to help you do the same. Sharing personal stories along with God's wisdom, Thelma invites you to join her on an easy-to-read journey out of depression. Interactive questions let you explore where you're at, and biblical insights and practical suggestions show you how to counter life's negativity by...

- discovering why God created you and loves you
- uncovering the positive truths about who you are
- developing a better knowledge of how Jesus can help you
- finding caring people who will listen and offer godly advice
- caring for yourself spiritually, emotionally, and physically

Thelma is a great traveling companion and encourager, making your path to good health positive and steady.

Worry and Anxiety Have to Go!

Are you anxious? Feeling concerned about your family, your job, your health, your finances? It's only natural, right? Dynamic author and speaker Thelma Wells says, "No!" When she discovered how to defeat worry and anxiety, she found a life of confident, joyful living. And she wants to help you experience more happiness too.

Offering hope and compassion, she invites you on an interactive journey that includes questions to help you evaluate your worries, biblical wisdom to give you strength, and doable steps to kick anxiety out of your life. Together you will...

- remove worry's mask of normalcy
- evaluate the impact of big and little worries in your life
- explore how faith in Christ will help you conquer anxiety
- discover how to stop anxiety as soon as it appears
- find ways to add upbeat, life-building thoughts to every day

Ready to Win™ *over Worry and Anxiety* reveals how you can eliminate worry and anxiety and choose freedom and peace in Christ.

Don't Give In...
God Wants YOU to Win!
God's Armor—Thelma Style

PREPARING FOR VICTORY IN THE BATTLE OF LIFE

THELMA WELLS

God Calls You "Winner"!

Is stress, indecision, heartache, or fear zapping your energy? Popular speaker and author Thelma Wells says life doesn't have to be that way! Opening her heart and God's Word, she reveals how God taught her to stand tall to win against discouragement and oppression by putting on God's armor. You'll discover...

- what spiritual warfare is
- who you're fighting
- what you're accomplishing

Thelma's contagious energy and enthusiasm invite you to tackle life with a "can do" attitude. You'll find great ways to dress for successful spiritual battle by:

- fixing your hair
  (putting on the helmet of salvation in Jesus for safety)
- padding your heart
  (donning the breastplate of righteousness to confront evil)
- putting on your stomping shoes
  (stepping out in faith against the devil)

No human wins every fight, so Thelma encourages you to call on Jesus when you get tired. He wants you to win, and He actively participates with you to ensure victory.

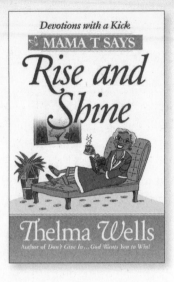

It's a Brand-new Day!

Dynamic, upbeat, and always forthright, author and popular speaker Thelma "Mama T" Wells encourages you to choose joy every day…and explains how to do that even when trouble turns your world upside down.

Through biblical wisdom and powerful stories that highlight God's amazing presence, extraordinary love, and unfailing provision, you'll soon embrace Thelma's steps to welcoming each day:

- never say "never" to God
- love and spend time with your family and friends
- be liberal with praise
- talk to God about everything
- dig into God's Word

From simple strategies to in-depth approaches, Mama T shows you how to draw closer to Jesus, experience the help He offers, and put joy and contentment into your day.